The genealogy of the Anglo-Norman Lynches who settled in Galway*

Paul B McNulty

* A partially updated version of my project submitted in partial fulfilment of the requirements for the National University of Ireland Diploma in Genealogy/Family History, Adult Education Centre, University College Dublin under the direction of Sean Murphy MA, Tutor, in June 2009. A peer-reviewed extract under the above title (but excluding the BrothersKeeper.com database) was published by the author in the
Journal of the Galway Archaeological and Historical Society, volume 62, 2010, pages 30-50.

Content

Figures

Figures (continued)

Tables

Appendices

Introduction

The invasion of Ireland by the Anglo-Normans in 1169 marked a seminal moment in Irish history. The invasion force was lead by Richard de Clare, better known as Strongbow, following an invitation from Dermot MacMurrough, the deposed king of Leinster. The Anglo-Norman position in Ireland was bolstered by the strategic marriage of Aoife, daughter of Dermot MacMurrough, to Strongbow in 1170. Shortly afterwards, Henry II, the Norman king of England also invaded Ireland to establish a Lordship of Ireland and to control Strongbow. This second invasion was justified by the English Pope, Adrian IV, in order to reform the allegedly corrupt religious practices in Ireland.[1]

Mostly from Wales, the Anglo-Normans soon created a substantial presence in Ireland that included the conquest of Connacht in 1235 by the de Burgos, de Lacys and Fitzgeralds. The language of their elite was a Norman dialect of French, which was gradually displaced by Gaelic and later by English. As such, the surname Lynch (originally *de Lench*) was Gaelicized to *Linseach* and later Anglicized to Lynch. The surname *de Lench* may be derived from the city of Linz in Austria. The continuing Anglo-Norman presence in modern Ireland is emphasized by the prominence of their surnames including those of Burke, Fitzgerald, Power, Barry, Roche and Butler in addition to Lynch.[2]

The precise origin of the Anglo-Norman Lynches who settled in Galway is difficult to establish. One source suggests that Andrew Lynch, a member of the invasion force, was the first Anglo-Norman Lynch in Ireland. He was provided with an estate in Summerhill (*Cnoc an Linsigh*), Co Meath by Henry II. His descendant, John, is reputed to have been the first Lynch to settle in Galway. John Lynch married the daughter of William de Lacy who died in battle in 1233. William was the son of the first Lord Deputy of Ireland, Hugh de Lacy. Hugh had married Rose, the daughter of Rory O'Connor, high king of Ireland, who had deposed Dermot MacMurrough, the king of Leinster. Hugh de Lacy granted William *le Petit* lands at Mullingar. It has been suggested that William *le Petit* was the ancestor of all the Lynches in Ireland and a 10th generational ancestor of Thomas Lynch, the provost of Galway. However, it is not possible to fit 10 generations between the arrival of the Anglo-Normans in Ireland in 1169 and the appointment of Thomas in 1274.[3]

Thus, it is not possible to determine whether Andrew or John Lynch or William *le Petit* is the ancestor of the Lynches of Galway. What we do know is that Thomas Lynch, the provost of Galway in 1274, married Bridget, daughter of the Lord Marshal, in 1280. They had two sons, James and William, from who are descended most of the Lynches recorded in pedigrees (Appendix 1, p 31). The senior line, sometimes referred to as Cranmore (*Crann Mór*), may be the line from the eldest son, James.[4]

---

[1]   F X Martin, 'The Normans: arrival and settlement, 1169-c.1300', p 95-112, in *The course of Irish history*, T W Moody and F X Martin, editors, Dublin, 2001; Art Cosgrove, editor, *A New History of Ireland, Vol.2, Medieval Ireland 1169-1534*, Oxford, 1987, 982 p.

[2]   Patrick Hanks and Flavia Hodges, *A Dictionary of Surnames*, Oxford, 1988, p 337; Sean J Murphy, A Survey of Irish Surnames 1993-97, http://homepage.eircom.net/%7Eseanjmurphy, viewed 1 May 2009.

[3]   M J Blake, *Blake family records, 1600-1700*, 2nd series, London, 1905, p 240, 241; Hugh de Lacy, http://www.britannica.com, Apr 2009; James Hardiman, 'The History of the Town and County of the Town of Galway', Dublin, 1820, p 17; William Playfair, *British Family Antiquity*, London, 1811, p 51-4.

[4]   M J Blake 'Account of the Lynch Family Written in 1815' *J Galway Arch Hist Soc*, vol 8, 1913-14, p 81-85; H. S Sweetman, editor, *Calendar of documents, Ireland*, 1171-1307, London, vol 1, p 53, 136; vol 2, p 344; M J Blake 'Pedigree of Lynch of Lavally' *J Galway Arch Hist Soc*, vol 10, 1917-18, p 66-69.

Whatever their source, the Lynches flourished within the walled town of Galway established by the Anglo-Normans (Figures 1 and 2, p 6). In 1312, Nicholas Lynch built the great gate of the town although he is not recorded in any of the known pedigrees. In 1484, Dominick Duff fitz John Lynch secured a charter for Galway from Richard III under which 'Mayors' were constituted. Dominick's brother, Peter Lynch, was the first mayor in 1485. In the same year, Pius VIII approved the transfer of the ecclesiastical control of the town of Galway from the diocese of Tuam to the newly constituted Wardenship of Galway. In 1493, Mayor James Lynch reputedly hanged his own son, Walter, who had murdered a young Spaniard named Gomez. Walter had thought that the Spaniard was befriending his girlfriend, Agnes. Both the story, and its association with the origin of the expression 'Lynch law', has been dismissed as fiction.[5]

In 1536, Henry VIII ordered Galwegians to shave their 'over-lips', grow hair to cover their ears, wear English-style clothes and learn to speak English.[6] Following Henry's break with Rome, the Irish Parliament abolished the papal Lordship of Ireland at his request. It was replaced by the kingdom of Ireland and was accompanied by the appointment of Henry VIII as the first English king of Ireland in 1541.

In 1610, the town (later the city) of Galway, including its immediate hinterland, was constituted as a separate county. The Lynches held the mayoralty of Galway on more than 80 occasions between 1485 and 1654. Elizabeth I appointed Roland Lynch as the Protestant bishop of Kilmacduagh in 1587 and of Clonfert in 1602. John fitz James Lynch was appointed as the Protestant Bishop of Elphin in 1583 although he is reputed to have died a papist.[7] His daughter, Mary, married Christopher, a brother of Sir Henry Lynch whose baronetcy of Ireland was created in 1622 by James I (Figure 3, p 7).

The tension that existed between the Anglo-Normans and the Gaelic Irish at the Confederation of Kilkenny preceded the conquest of Galway by the Cromwellians in 1652. After the conquest, the power-base of the Lynches and other Anglo-Norman families in Galway City was weakened and was eventually broken. The shift was illustrated by a meeting of the Council of Galway in 1686 wherein power was equally shared between representatives of the 14 Tribes of Galway (predominantly Anglo-Norman or old English) and the new arrivals (new English). The Lynches eventually migrated to the countryside. In due course, a property portfolio was assembled comprised of ten estates. A more recent analysis has categorized twenty Lynch families by location mostly in Co Galway but also in Co Mayo with a small presence in Co Roscommon.[8]

Notwithstanding their defeat in Galway City, the Lynches continued to make an important contribution in the national and international arena. Of the 17 Lynches, featured in the *Oxford Dictionary of National Biography*, seven of the 11 Irish-born were

---

[5] William Henry, *Role of Honour-The Mayors of Galway City 1485-2001*, Galway, 2002, p 29-33; Edward MacLysaght, 'Report on documents relating to the Wardenship of Galway' *Analecta Hibernica*, 1944, vol 14, p 1-249; T P O'Neill, 'Surnames of County Galway' *Irish Roots*, 1994 (1) 26-28.

[6] J T Gilbert, *Archives of the Town of Galway*, Hist Mss Comm, 10th Report, App V, London, 1885, p 380.

[7] James Morrin, *Calendar of the patent rolls Ireland: Elizabeth V (18th -45th year)*, Dublin, vol 2, 1862.

[8] P J Corish, 'Two contemporary historians of the confederation of Kilkenny: John Lynch and Richard O'Ferrell' *Ir Histl Studies*, vol 8, p 217-236; John Lowe, *Letter-Book of the Earl of Clanricarde 1643-47*, IMC, Dublin, 1983, 504 p; Patrick Melvin, 'The Galway Tribes as Landowners and Gentry', in *Galway History and Society*, Dublin, 1996, p 331; Lynch estates, http://www.landedestates.ie, Mar 2009.

descendants of the Anglo-Norman Lynches who settled in Galway: namely, Richard Lynch (1610–1676), Jesuit and theologian; John Lynch (*d*. circa 1677), historian; Dominick Lynch (1622–1697), Dominican theologian; James Lynch (1626–1713), Roman Catholic archbishop of Tuam; Henry Blosse Lynch (1807–1873), explorer in Mesopotamia; Patrick Edward Lynch (1810–1884), army officer; and Thomas Ker Lynch (1818–1891), explorer in Mesopotamia.[9]

The Lynches also emigrated to various countries including Argentina, France and the West Indies. The 1678 census for the island of Montserrat, West Indies recorded ten Galwegian Lynches as early planters and merchants.[10] Recorded among the slaveholding planters and merchants in Montserrat in 1730 were Bartholomew Lynch (50 slaves) and Catherine Lynch (46 slaves). After the abolition of slavery in 1834, some slaves adopted the surnames of their former Irish owners.

The Lynches have been described as an aloof aristocracy marrying within their own circle. They were intensely loyal to the English crown and some found it difficult to cope with the campaigns for land reform and Home Rule that emerged in the late 19th century. The social conditions of their impoverished tenantry were feudal.[11]

My interest in the genealogy of the Lynches arose, firstly, from a study of my wife's family, the Conneelys of Lettermullen, Connemara, in which Nicholas Lynch of Barna, Co Galway was identified as their landlord in 1829.[12] Secondly, the marriage of Patrick Lynch of Tuam to Bridget Higgins, the daughter of my maternal grandaunt, Mary McHugh, established a personal relationship with a Lynch family of Galway. Thirdly, a connection with my maternal grandmother, Mary Fallon, of the Fallons of Turloughmore, Co Galway was suggested by various Fallon-Lynch marriages. The marriages include that of Joanna, daughter of Oliver Lynch reputedly Mayor of Galway in 1503 to John 'O' Fallon; and the 1865 marriage of Cecilia, daughter of Thomas Lynch of Lavally, to John Fallon of Netterville Lodge, Mountbellew, Co Galway. The allocation of 107 Irish acres in the barony of Kilconnell, Co Galway to John Fallon and his wife Annable of Derrycahell, Roscommon in 1654-58 may be relevant as my Fallon relatives are believed to have originated in that barony.[13]

This study will focus on validating, extending and integrating the Lynch pedigrees to provide a genealogy that will be available on-line. Of particular interest is the assertion that the Lynches, unlike the Blakes, cannot be traced back to a common ancestor.[14]

The BrothersKeeper.com database
The Anglo-Norman Lynches who settled in Galway have been entered onto a BrothersKeeper.com genealogy database using documented pedigrees as source.[15] At

---

[9]   'Lynch' in *Oxford Dictionary of National Biography*, http://www.oxforddnb.com/index.jsp, 6 Mar 2009.

[10]   Brian McGinn, 'How Irish is Montserrat?' *Irish Roots*, 1994, (1), p 20-23; (2), p 15-17; (4), p 20-21.

[11]   C H Lynch-Robinson, *The last of the Irish R M's*, London, p 23-4.

[12]   Tithe Applotment, Microfilm 38, Kilcummin parish 11/23, p 14, National Archives, Dublin.

[13]   Gerarda McHugh, 'Lynch's Mill at Bodane' in *Sylane National School 1852-2002*, p 111-113, NUI Galway Library; M J Blake 'An Old Lynch Manuscript', p 93 and 'Pedigree of Lynch of Lavally, Co Galway' p 66-69; Robert C Simington, *The Transplantation to Connacht 1654-58*, Irish Manuscripts Commission, Dublin, 1970, p 124.

[14]   Patrick Melvin, 'The Galway Tribes as Landowners and Gentry', p 330.

[15]   John Steed, *Brother's Keeper®, version 6.2, Genealogy program for Windows*, Michigan, 2005.

this time, 2843 individuals comprising 1234 families have been entered onto the database. The largest group of 1726 individuals is comprised of the Anglo-Norman Lynches demonstrating that it has been possible to connect most of the documented pedigrees entered onto a database that is available on-line. All the members of this group can be traced back to a common ancestor, Thomas Lynch, the provost of Galway in 1274, notwithstanding a contention to the contrary. The next largest group of 628 individuals represents the author's ancestors and relations bearing the predominantly Gaelic surnames of Conneely, Fallon, Farrell, Griffin, McDonagh, McHugh, McNulty and O'Brien apart from Cooke and possibly Lynch (Database, p 57-149). The Lynch surname could be either Anglo-Norman or Gaelic. No connection between the Lynch and Fallon relatives of the author with the Anglo-Norman Lynches has yet been found.

There are also some smaller Anglo-Norman Lynch groups that have not as yet been connected to the largest database group. These include the extended family of Stanislaus Lynch of Galway, Chief Land Commissioner, 1885 (93 people); the Lynches of Lydican, Claregalway, Co Galway who are one of the ancestors of 'Che' Guervara (36 people); the Lynches of Garracloon, Cong, Co Mayo, one of the ancestors of 'Bram' Stoker, the author of *Dracula* (33 people); and Captain Stephen Lynch of Galway and Paris who was related to those involved in the infamous Bodkin massacre (28 people).[16]

Prior to entry of individuals onto the database, the pedigrees were scrutinized to ensure that the recorded relationships were substantiated by documentary evidence as far as possible. In general, the documentary evidence becomes more elusive as the investigation stretches back in time. In most cases, Irish pedigrees can be traced back to the early 19th century using a variety of genealogical sources including records of births, marriages and deaths supplemented by census and property valuation records. The more affluent members of society can be traced further back because records of births, marriages and deaths were supplemented by other genealogical records including wills and deeds. This applies to the Anglo-Norman Lynches who settled in Galway some of whom prospered as merchants in Galway City and later as landed gentry after their expulsion from the city by Cromwell in 1652. Particularly good records are available for the baronetical Lynches (later Lynch-Blosse) as one would expect for an a titled family created by James I in 1622 (Figure 4, p 7).

The individuals in the various Lynch pedigrees were entered onto a BrothersKeeper.com database and later transferred to Ancestry.com. Individuals were identified by a question mark between their first and last name where doubt existed as to the veracity of the relationship. For example, Thomas ? Lynch has been recorded as the son of Dominick Lynch, Mayor of Galway in 1580.[17] However, Thomas ? Lynch is not recorded in a 1587 deed in which his reputed father, Mayor Dominick Lynch, settled

---

[16] M J Blake 'Some former Lynch families of Co Galway-ancestry of Stanislaus Lynch and his relations' *Tuam Herald*, 1, 8, 15 Dec 1928, pages 4; Brian McGinn, 'Che Guevara's Irish blood, The Lynch family of Argentina' *Ir Roots*, 1993 (2) 11-14; Paul Murray, *From the shadow of Dracula: A life of Bram Stoker*, 2004, p 8, 9; Jarlath O'Connell, *The Bodkin murders*, http://places.galwaylibrary.ie/history/chapter77.html.

[17] Pedigree of Lynch afterwards Lynch Blosse of Castlecarra, Clogher, Co Mayo and of Cadiz in Spain, 1250-c.1812, Ms 170, NLI, p 135-139; Pedigree of Lynch of Athenry, Drimcong, Ballydavid, Lydican and Lynch's Grove, Co Galway and of Paris, c.1430-1784, Ms 165, NLI, p 389-392; M J Blake, 'An Old Lynch Manuscript' *J Galway Arch Hist Soc, vol* 8, 1913-1914, p 70 and 'Pedigree of Lynch of Lavally'.

his estate among his five sons, John, Nicholas, Stephen, Geoffrey and Henry. Because of the conflict of evidence, Thomas ? Lynch has been entered with a question mark and an explanatory note in his database entry. A double slash, //, signifying uncertainty, has been entered on any pedigree line linking Dominick to Thomas ? Lynch (Appendix 2, p 32).

The names of the individuals were entered as recorded onto the database except where substantial numbers of variant names were encountered. In these cases, standardization of name format was necessary to avoid duplication of entries, to cluster families together (Database, p 57-149) and to facilitate the connection of pedigrees. Nevertheless, variant names were retained by moving them into the space between the forename and the surname as the database only searches for the first and last name entered. For example, Maria was standardised as Mary 'Maria' and Robuck as Robert 'Robuck'. Thus, Robert 'Robuck' (2nd Bt) Lynch will be retrieved when 'Robert Lynch' is searched, along with the nine other Robert Lynches in the database. The issue of the two Anglicized forms, Bourke and Burke, of the Anglo-Norman *de Burgh* or *de Burgo* surname has been resolved by selecting the more commonly accepted form, Burke,[18] and by entering the more upper-class Bourke as 'Bourke' Burke. The issue of Argentinian surnames has been resolved by renaming *Ernesto Che Guevara de la Serna* by Che 'de la Serna' Guevara which can be searched as 'Che Guevara' or as '? Guevara'.

Multiple sequential spouses among the landed gentry of Galway and Mayo were not unusual. Thomas Lynch (d.1419) of Galway has been recorded as married to Joanna Penrise both as first and second wife.[19] His first wife has also been reported as unknown and his second wife as Rosa Dillon. A further complication has arisen because Stephen Lynch has been recorded as a son of both Joanna Penrise and Rosa Dillon. One explanation is that Thomas Lynch had three wives, the first unknown followed by Joanna Penrise, followed by Rosa Dillon, and that both Joanna and Rosa had sons named Stephen (Appendix 2, p 32). This model has been entered onto the database.

Pedigrees varied greatly in the extent of familial information provided. Most pedigrees focused on establishing inheritance rights usually exercised through the oldest surviving son. However, more extensive familial information was provided occasionally from which it emerged that large families were not unusual among the landed gentry. Some were unusually large, possibly, a response to a high rate of infant mortality. Nicholas Lynch, Mayor of Galway in 1584 had 12 sons, at least four of whom died in infancy. His 12th son, Christopher, married Mary, the daughter of John Lynch, Bishop of Elphin, and they parented four sons and nine daughters. Their four sons, John, Lazarus, Anthony and Thomas, and one of their daughters, Evelyn, died as infants. Jennet French bore 13 children to Alderman Anthony Lynch of Galway, who died in 1638 (Figure 5, p 8). Seven of her eleven boys died young, two of them named Thomas. Alicia, the extraordinary daughter of Martin Browne of Claran, Headford, Co Galway, bore 16 sons to Thomas Lynch of Headford, Co Galway whom she had married in 1840.[20]

---

[18]   Edward MacLysaght, *The Surnames of Ireland*, 5th edition, Dublin, 1980, p 22, 30.

[19]   Ms 170, p 135; M J Blake 'An Old Lynch Manuscript' *J Galway Arch Hist Soc*, vol 9, 1915-16, p 79-107 and 'Pedigree of Lynch of Lavally'.

[20]   Lynch of Galway, Betham Sketch Pedigrees I, IV, GO, NLI Ms 264, p 45-50; Lynch, Christopher (d.1635), Funeral Entry, Ms 69, 1638, p 342, NLI; M J Blake 'Unpublished pedigrees of Lynch families-Lynch of Mount Ross, Headford and Lynch of Ballycurren', *Tuam Herald*, 22, 29 Dec 1928, p 4.

1. Map of Galway town *circa* 1651 (north is to the viewer's left).[21]

2. Lynch's castle, Galway, *c.*1500 built of limestone in the Irish gothic style and noted for its elaborate decorative style. Bearing the arms of Henry VII and the Lynch family, it is now occupied by the AIB bank at the junction of Shop and Abbeygate Streets.[22]

---

[21]   William Henry, *Role of Honour-The Mayors of Galway City 1485-2001.*
[22]   Art Cosgrove, *A New History of Ireland. Vol.2, Medieval Ireland 1169-1534*, plate 17a.

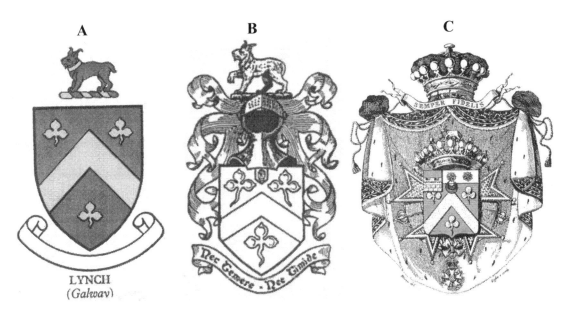

3. Arms A, Lynch (Galway);[23] B, Lynch-Blosse, *Nec temere, nec timide* ('Neither rashly, nor timidly'), created for Sir Henry Lynch, Galway, 1st Baronet, 1622;[24] Arms C, Count Jean Baptiste Lynch, Bordeaux, *Semper fidelis* ('Always faithful'), created 1814.[25]

4. Unidentified portraits of the Anglo-Norman Lynches found in Galway (possibly Sir Henry Lynch-Blosse, 7th Bt, left, and his nephew, Sir Robert Lynch-Blosse, 8th Bt), courtesy of Constance Mabel Frances Bate (*nee* Lynch-Blosse) and Richard Hely Lynch-Blosse, 17th Bt.

23   Edward MacLysaght, *Irish Families: Their Names, Arms and Origins*, Dublin, 1957, p 213-4, Plate 19.

24   *Burke's Peerage and Baronetage* Switzerland, 107th ed, 2003, vol 2, Lynch-Blosse, p 2436.

25   Bernadette Ní Loingsigh, 'Loingsigh Bhordeaux' *Galvia*, 1960, vol 7, p 2 and 14.

'Anthony Linch of the town of Galway, Alderman, 6th son of the same (*recte* James)[26] Alderman, eldest son and heir of Ambrose Linch of the same Alderman. The said Anthony took to wife Jennet, daughter of Nicholas French of the same, Alderman, by whom he had issue, 10 sons and 3 daughters, vidz, Martin, eldest son and heir, who took to wife Mary, daughter of Andrew Linch of Beallabanchir? in the county of Galway, gent; Henry 2nd son; Thomas 3rd son; Michael 4th son; Andrew 5th son; Anthony 6th son; John 7th son; Thomas 8th son; all 7 died young and unmarried; William 10th son married to daughter of Marcus Skerrett of Galway aforesaid Burgess; Mary eldest daughter of the said Anthony married to Dominick Linch of Galway Burgess; Jennett 2nd daughter married to Dominick Darcy of Galway gent; Margaret 3rd daughter married to Valentine Frinch of Galway gent. The said Anthony departed this mortal life at Galway aforesaid the ? of November 1638 & was interred in St Francis Abbey near Galway …'

5. Funeral Entry for Alderman Anthony Lynch (d.1638), eldest son and heir of Alderman James Lynch of Galway (lower case 's' is written as 'f') including a partial transcription.[27]

---

[26]   Genealogical Office Ms 264, National Library of Ireland, p 45-50; Will of Anthony Lynch, in Arthur Vicars, *Index to the Prerogative Wills of Ireland 1536-1810*, Dublin, 1897, 512 p.

[27]   Alderman Anthony Lynch, Funeral Entry, GO Ms 70, vol 7, p 547, National Library of Ireland.

Stephen Lynch of Gallway Esquire sometyme Recordor there — sonne of Nicholas Lynch of Galloway aforesaid Esquire, which Stephen tooke to wife Katherin daughter of Robert Blake of Galloway aforesaid and by her had issue two sonnes and five daughters vidz. Nicholas and Thomas, and Anstace, Katherin Mary Iulian and Ioane, The said first mentioned Stephen departed this mortall life at Galloway the aforesaid the 26th of Nouember 1636. and was interred in the parish Church of St Nicholas the 29th of the same Monneth The trueth of the premiss is testified by the subscription of the said Katherin Relict & Executrix of the said defunct Whoe hath returned this Certificat into my office to be there recorded, Taken by me Thomas Preston Esquire Vluester King of Armes this 14th of Iuly 1639.

Catherin Lynche

Nicholas (Mayor) Lynch—Stephen Lynch—Nicholas Lynch
                m. Catherine Blake —Thomas Lynch
                —Anastacia 'Anstace' Lynch
                —Catherine Lynch
                —Mary Lynch
                —Julia 'Julian' Lynch
                —Joan 'Joane' Lynch

6. Funeral Entry for Stephen Lynch (d.1636), Recorder of Galway, sixth son of Nicholas Lynch, Mayor of Galway in 1584 (lower case 's' is written as 'f') and an associated BrothersKeeper.com pedigree chart.[28]

---

28   Genealogical Office Ms 70, vol 7, p 30, National Library of Ireland.

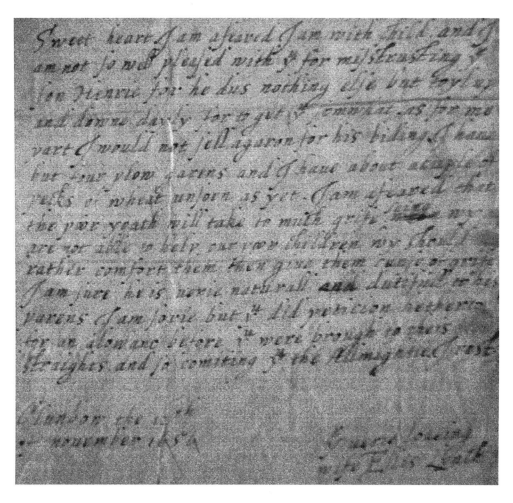

'For my dearest Cusen Sir Robuck Lynch these at Gallway'

Sweet Heart I am afeared I am with child and I am not so well pleased with you for mistrusting your son Henrie for he dus nothing else but toyl up and downe dayly for to get you somewhat. As for me part I would not sell a garan for his biding. I have but four plow garrens and I have about a cuple of pecks of wheat unsown as yet. I am afeared that the poor yoath will take to much grife. Seing wy are not able to help our poor children wy should rather comfort them than give them cause of grife. I am sure he is verie naturall and dutifull to his parens. I am sorie but you did peticion hetherto for an alowance before you were brought to theis straights and so comiting you the Allmightie I rest,

Clunbow the 12th
Your verie loveing of November 1656
wife Ellis Lynch

7. Letter from Ellis French to her husband, Robert 'Robuck' Lynch, 2nd Bt, with reference to their eldest son, Henry, destined to succeed his father as 3rd Bt.[29]

---

[29] Original letter courtesy of Richard Hely Lynch-Blosse, 17th Bt; transcription of letter, K W Nicholls, 'The Lynch Blosse Papers', *Analecta Hibernica,* 1980, vol 29, item 6, p 120.

8. Record of the appointment of Thomas Blake, 2nd Bt as Mayor of Galway, 1637;
Marcus Lynch fitz William as Sheriff; James Lynch fitz Stephen as Sheriff;
and Thomas Lynch as Recorder.[30]

9. Hely Richard Lynch-Blosse (1887-1928) photographed at Harrow school, London in
sporting dress in 1901-1906 flanked by his father, Edward F Lynch-Blosse (1853-1926)
of Wales, and mother, Edith Caroline Walker of Sussex (d.1953).[31]

---

[30]   Galway Corporation statute book (*Liber A*) 1485-1709, NUI Galway, Special Collections LA1.
[31]   Photograph 001149, negative 18469, H R Bloss-Lynch, http://www.harrowphotos.com/;
Photographs of parents, courtesy of Craig Lynch-Blosse, calb@ihug.co.nz.

10. Richard Hely Lynch-Blosse as a boy with his mother, Elizabeth Payne, his sister, Caroline Susan, and his father, David Edward Lynch-Blosse, 16th Bt (d.1971) (courtesy of Richard Hely Lynch-Blosse, 17th Bt, of Oxfordshire).

11. The extended Lynch-Blosse (L-B) family at the former home of Valerie Lynch-Blosse (Cormack) at Great Missendon, Buckinghamshire *circa* 2000.
Those bearing the birth surname of Lynch-Blosse are identified by their first name only, except in some cases where the surname of a partner is given in parentheses (courtesy of Richard Hely Lynch-Blosse, 17th Bt).

Back row (from left): Valerie, David, Valerie's daughter and husband (Cormack), Caroline, Peter Barry, Jean Hair (L-B), Margaret (Couper), Robert Sullivan-Tailyour, Hannah, Jen Hall, not known, Josephine Blosse-Stuart, Richard 17th Bt, Bridget (Barry), George Richardson, Mrs Bate-Williams, Robert, Alana, John Bullock, Janet Couper (Onelik), Archie Couper (Moira's husband);

Seated (from left): Oliver, Hugh, Katherine, Craig, Jamie Hall, Elizabeth 'Beth' Payne (L-B), Efa Blosse-Mason, Jacob Blosse-Rollnick, Peggy Richardson, Valerie (Bullock), Iris (Dare), Sylvia (Sullivan-Tailyour) and Moira Hunt (Couper);

On grass (from left): Charlie Blosse Barry and not known.

12. The house of the Lynches of Clogher, Claremorris, Co Mayo, *c.*1798-1860s.[32]

13. Partry house, Ballinrobe, Co Mayo home of the Blosse-Lynches, 1667-*c.*1990.[33]

14. Athavallie house, Balla, Co Mayo, home of the Lynch-Blosses, *c.*1800-1909.[34]

---

[32]   Photograph, sales catalogue, 24/27, Apr 1967, Irish Architectural Archive; http://www.landedestates.ie.
[33]   Property supplement, editor, Jack Fagan, *Irish Times*, 26 April 1990.
[34]   Athavallie house, Balla, Co Mayo, photograph 2003, Irish Architectural Archive.

15. Mrs Kelly, c.1820, daughter of Nicholas Lynch of Barna and Catherine Blake of Ballinakill, Renvyle, Co Galway. 'Mrs Kelly wears a high-waisted dress with a low, v-shaped décolletage, short sleeves with unusual, long muslin undersleeves and a gothic lace band at the neckline.' The oil on canvas portrait, NGI 1270, has been attributed to Martin Archer Shee, 1769-1850.[35]

16. The house of the Lynches of Barna, Co Galway, 1656?-c.1930.[36]

---

[35] Nicola Figgis and Brendan Rooney, *Irish Paintings in the National Gallery of Ireland*, vol 1, 2001.

[36] Barna house, Co Galway, photograph, 022/013, Irish Architectural Archive.

17. The home of the Lynches of Cloghballymore, Kilcolgan, Co Galway, 1767-*c*.1855.[37]

18. 'Lynch's House at Shrule', Ballinrobe, Co Mayo[38]

19. Originally a Staunton property, Waterdale house, Claregalway, Co Galway, was leased by John Wilson Lynch from 1857 to 1870. His uncles, George and Henry Lynch, adopted the surname, Lynch-Staunton.[39]

---

[37] Cloghballymore castle and mansion, Co Galway, photograph, *c*.1910, Irish Architectural Archive.

[38] C C Ormsby, 'The Castle and Lynch's House (so called) at Shrule' *J Galway Arch Hist Soc*, vol 8, 1913-1914, p 224-226 including a note by M J Blake.

[39] Waterdale house, Claregalway, Co Galway, photograph, 022/095, Irish Architectural Archive.

Validation of entries on database

A 'quality' check of 2843 individuals comprising 1234 families on the author's BrothersKeeper.com database revealed some minor errors that have been corrected apart from a 16th century section in the Moore pedigree that still needs attention. A 'reasonableness' check is based on setting minimum and maximum ages for certain events and then checking if people lie within the range specified. The database default settings (years) were: marriage (12-90), death (0-99), age of father at childbirth (14-80), age of mother at childbirth (14-50) and age difference of spouses (0-30). The result of one of the 27 cases was:

Geoffrey Lynch, born c.~~1618~~ 1617 Age of father, Dominick = ~~10~~ 20y, born c.~~1607~~ 1597

Errors have been highlighted by a strike-through and their replacement by better estimates. Specifically, Dominick Lynch if born *circa* 1607 would have been too young to be the father of Geoffrey, born *circa* 1618. Their dates of birth had been estimated from the designation of their younger brothers as the eldest minors in the wills of their respective fathers in 1627 and 1638.[40] Appropriate adjustments were made so that Dominick would have been about 20 years old when he fathered Geoffrey.

The foregoing example highlights the importance of wills as a source to validate entries in a genealogical database. For example, the 1499 will of Valentine Blake of Galway has been used to confirm the contemporaneous existence of: 1. Dominick fitz John Lynch, Mayor of Galway who died in 1508; 2. James Lynch, whose father, Sir Geoffrey Walter Lynch, had been Mayor of Galway *circa* 1488; and 3. Stephen fitz Dominick Lynch, the Mayor of Galway who died in 1531.[41]

Analysis of prerogative wills has revealed 61 individual entries for the descendants of the Anglo-Norman Lynches who settled in Galway. Of these, 19 were identified as the wills of Lynches already entered onto the author's database most of which had been used as source material in the preparation of the pedigree of the particular person. Similar remarks apply to the testamentary card index (1701-1904) which revealed 21 individual entries and to the Crossle genealogical abstracts (1680-1790) which revealed 16 individual entries for the descendants of the Anglo-Norman Lynches who settled in Galway.[42]

Funeral entries have also been used in the preparation of family pedigrees. Those recorded in the 17th century are of particular interest due to the high quality of the recorded script and their easy readability on microfilm (Figures 5 and 6, p 8 and 9). The human face of the people recorded in 17th century pedigrees has been revealed in a series of letters among the baronetical Lynches (Figure 7, p 10).

On-line state papers covering the Tudor period from 1509 to 1603 were searched

---

[40]   M J Blake 'An Old Lynch Manuscript' p 71, 72; Arthur Vicars, *Index to the Prerogative Wills of Ireland 1536-1810*.

[41]   M J Blake, *Blake family records, 1300-1600*, 1st series, London, 1902, Record 69, p 47-49; 'Indexes to Clonfert Marriage Licence Bonds, Wills and Administration Bonds', supplement to *Irish Ancestor*, 1970, National Library of Ireland; P Beryl Eustace, *Registry of Deeds Dublin: Abstracts of Wills, Vol II, 1746-85*, Irish Manuscripts Commission, Dublin, 1954, p 32, 33.

[42]   Arthur Vicars, *Index to the Prerogative Wills of Ireland 1536-1810*; Crossle Genealogical Abstracts and Testamentary card indices, National Archives of Ireland; Will, William Linche, Southampton, 1614 in *Genealogical memoranda relating to the family of Lynch*, 1883, p 13, http://www.archive.org, May 2009.

for information on the Lynches of Galway. Only four records and five index entries were recovered when 'Lynch' was searched. However, 32 records and 29 index entries were recovered when 'Lynche' was searched. Regrettably, little information of genealogical importance was uncovered as evident from the following examples. A petition to retain Captain Henry Clare as commander of HM forces in Galway city was signed in 1601 by Mayor Christopher fitz George Lynch, bailiff Nicholas Lynch, bailiff Robert Blake and alderman Anthony Lynch among other prominent citizens. The mayoral and bailiff appointments have been confirmed by Hardiman. The only Christopher Lynch (d.1635) on the author's database is the 12th son of Mayor Nicholas Lynch and therefore Mayor Christopher fitz George Lynch is a different person whose father, George, is unknown. Furthermore, no linkage to the Lynch database was found in the case of Janet Lynch, farmer of a water-mill in Galway and Thomas Martyn of Galway town who owed tax for netting salmon in 1537.[43]

Analysis of Lynches indexed in relevant publications has yielded valuable genealogical information. Lynches of Gaelic origin have been indexed in *The Great Book of Irish Genealogies* both as a surname *Ó Loinsigh* and as a personal name *Loinseach*. *Ó Loinsigh* is indexed 22 times from 985 to 1159 well before the advent of the Anglo-Norman Lynches in 1169.[44] In contrast, Anglo-Norman Lynches have not been indexed in *The Great Book of Irish Genealogies* or in the *Annals of the Four Masters* but are well documented in various state calendars. In 1583, John Lynch was appointed as Protestant Bishop of Elphin by Elizabeth I thus corroborating his entry in various Lynch pedigrees. He and his colleague, Roland Lynch, Bishop of Kilmacduagh were directed to encourage the sons of English speaking gentry to study at Oxford and Cambridge in the expectation that they would become Protestant chaplains and schoolmasters. In 1591, a pardon was extended to Nicholas Linch fitz Stephen, Robuck Linch fitz Nicholas, Chr Linch fitz George, and Marcus Linch fitz Stephen of Galway, one of 41 indexed Lynch entries.[45]

The 41 Lynches indexed in *Galway History and Society* correspond to 53 individuals.[46] All were cross-referenced with database Lynches except for 17 individuals suggesting that their genealogy has not been documented or that their records have not survived. For example, three of the six indexed John Lynches were not identified among the 46 database John Lynches (Database, p 109, p 111).

From 1485 through 1654, more than 80 Mayors of Galway bearing the surname, Lynch, were elected. Only 26 Mayors have been identified in genealogical sources. The various John Lynches who served as Mayor in 1489, 1494, 1543, 1551, 1552 and 1572 have not been identified among the 46 database John Lynches. Members of the Lynch sept were also prominent among the annual appointments of sheriffs and recorders. For example, James Lynch fitz Stephen was appointed as a sheriff in 1637 (Figure 8, page

---

[43]   'Lynch', Records 1-30, 'Lynche', records 31, 32, Letters and Papers, Foreign and Domestic, of Henry VIII;   Calendar   Mss   Salisbury,   State   Papers   Online,   Part   1, http://go.galegroup.com/mss/basicSearch.do, Mar 2009; James Hardiman 'The History of the Town and County of the Town of Galway', p 221.

[44]   Nollaig O Muraile, editor, *The great book of Irish genealogies*, Dublin, 2003, vol 4, p 143, 144; vol 5, p 436, 437; John O'Donovan, *Annals of the Four Masters*, vol 7, Index, Dublin, 1851, p 345, 346.

[45]   James Morrin, *Calendar of the patent rolls Ireland: Elizabeth V (18th -45th year)*, p 66; H C Hamilton, *Calendar of state papers, Ireland: 1588-1592, 1592-1596*, London, 1885, p 450; *The Irish Fiants of the Tudor Sovereigns*, vol 3, Queen Elizabeth I, 1586-1603; vol 4, Index-Elizabeth, Dublin, 1994.

[46]   Gerard Moran, R Gillespie and Wm Nolan, ed *Galway: History & Society*, Dublin, 1996, p 827-8.

11).[47] A database search failed to positively identify him among three of 20 James Lynches whose father was Stephen (Database, p 107, p 109). The only contemporaneous entry was that for a James Lynch fitz Stephen who might have been a nephew of Alderman Anthony Lynch who died in 1638. He might also have been one of five James Lynches whose father was unknown. A similar unsuccessful search was encountered for Marcus Lynch fitz William, the other sheriff appointed in 1637.

1. Religious persuasion of the Anglo-Norman Lynches whose ancestors settled in Galway as gleaned from selected marital records in the 19th century.[48]

Bride	Groome	Date	Church
Jeanette Victoir Lynch	Abraham F Royse	c.1830	COI, Galway
Barbara Lynch	Lt Col Geoghegan	1851	RC (not in GRO)
Horatia Anne Rushworth	Marcus S Lynch-Staunton	1851	RC (not in GRO)
Michael Lynch	Anne Lewen	1851	COI, Tuam
Harriett Browne	Robt Lynch-Blosse 10th Bt	1853	COI
Ellen Lynch	Edward Thomas Stapleton	1855	RC (not in GRO)
Victoire Corbet	Francis H Lynch-Staunton	1857	Protestant, Canada
Margaret Buckle	Randal E Lynch Athy	1858	RC (not in GRO)
Jane Joyce	Henry Lynch	1860	RC (not in GRO)
Mary Anne Lynch-Staunton	John Blake	1861	RC (not in GRO)
Cecilia Lynch	John Fallon	1865	RC, Dublin
Frances Redington	John Wilson Lynch	1865	RC, Oranmore
Henrietta Darcy	Anthony Lynch	1872	RC, Dublin
Helena Mary Nugent	Richard Charles Lynch	1876	RC, Delvin
Annie Stokes	Henry Lynch-Blosse 11Bt	1881	COE, Chelsea
Annette Frances Gradwell	Edmond J P Lynch Athy	1881	RC, Portumna
Mary Carwardine Walker	Rev Robert Lynch-Blosse	1881	COE, Sussex
Harriet Lynch-Blosse	Henry A Robinson, 1st Bt	1883	COE, Kent
Edith Caroline Walker	Edward F Lynch-Blosse	1883	COE, Sussex.
Ana 'y Ortiz' Lynch	Roberto 'Castro' Guevara	1884	RC, Argentina
M Constance Lynch-Blosse	Robert Nicholas Hardinge	1892	COE, Islington
Alice G N Pery-Knox-Gore	Robert Lynch-Blosse 12Bt	1893	COI, Dublin,
Frieda Ottman	Sir John Patrick Lynch	1896	COI
Kathleen Mary Lynch	Capt Denis Daly	1899	RC, Dublin

The religious persuasion of the Anglo-Norman Lynches who settled in Galway appears to have been equally distributed between Roman Catholic (13) and Protestant (11) during the 19th century (Table 1, above). It seems that the Anglo-Normans were

---

[47] William Henry, *Role of Honour-The Mayors of Galway City 1485-2001*, p 217, 218; Galway Corporation statute book (*Liber A*) 1485-1709.
[48] Marriages 1845-1899, General Register Office, Dublin 1; Brigid Clesham, *The register of the parish of St Nicholas, (Church of Ireland) Galway, 1792-1840*, Dublin, 2005, 163 p; Henry Farrar, *Index to Irish Marriages, 1771-1812*, London, 1897.

generally content to remain Catholic until the Cromwellian settlement (1652), and the subsequent Penal Laws (1691-1778), persuaded many to conform to Protestantism so that they could retain their privileges and property. The freedom to resume Catholicism became possible following Catholic emancipation in 1829. Thus, it was not surprising that Richard, son of Charles Lynch of Petersburgh, married Helena Mary Nugent in a Roman Catholic church even though his great great-grandfather, Sir Peter Lynch, had conformed in 1765 despite his papal knighthood. However, his conversion to Protestantism has been described as a 'feigned act of conformity'. In similar fashion, Andrew Crean (1705-) has been described as the 'sham conformist of Boulabeg'. He adopted the surname Crean-Lynch following his marriage to Mary, daughter and heiress of Dominick Lynch of Newborough House, Kilbennan, Tuam and also acquired that property. Edmond Lynch of Kilconla conformed in 1738 and may possibly be related to my relatives, the Catholic Lynches of Bodane, Kilconly, Tuam, Co Galway.[49]

On-line newspapers were scrutinized to validate genealogical information. Particular attention was focused on the baronetical Lynch-Blosses in *The Irish Times* which yielded 101 Lynch-Blosse entries over the period 1859 to 2003. Some minor corrections and additional information were noted. Edward F Lynch-Blosse of Glamorgan, the grandson of Robert Lynch-Blosse, 8th Bt, was photographed in 1910 at the Albert College farm, Glasnevin, Dublin (Figure 9, p 11). His eldest son, Henry Lynch-Blosse, 15th Bt, the Welsh mining expert, advised on Irish mining in 1944. His third son, Hely Richard, is the grandfather of Richard Hely Lynch-Blosse, 17th Bt, a general practitioner in Oxfordshire (Figures 10 and 11, p 12). His fourth son, Cecil Eagles, is the grandfather of David Ian Lynch-Blosse, the baronetical heir presumptive. His sixth son was the famous pilot, Patrick Windsor Lynch-Blosse, who flew from England to Australia and back in 1933 (Database, p 123).[50]

Descendants of James, son of Thomas Lynch (Provost of Galway, 1274)

Most Lynch pedigrees derive from the two great descendant lines of James and William, the sons of Thomas Lynch, Provost of Galway in 1274 (Appendix 1, p 31). The descendant line of James de Lynch leads to the pedigrees of the Lynches of Antigua, Cadiz, Clogher (Figure 12, p 13), Corrandulla and Castlecarra, Drimcong, Dughiska (Merlin Park), Lydican, Partry (Figure 13, p 13) and Petersburg; and to Crean-Lynch of Hollybrook and Lynch-Blosse of Castlecarra. A descendant register book for James Lynch is comprised of 317 descendants and 161 spouses. These constitute 106 families over 23 generations to the present, corresponding to a generational period of 32 years.

The first nine generations of the pedigree of James de Lynch concludes with the family of Nicholas Lynch, Mayor of Galway in 1584 (Appendix 3, p 33). His fourth son, Sir Henry Lynch, was appointed to a Baronetcy in 1622. After the expulsion of the

---

[49]   Moody and Martin, *The course of Irish history*, p 176-189; Eileen O'Byrne and Anne Chamney, *The convert rolls, 1703-1838*, IMC, Dublin, 2005, p 384, 385; Newborough House, Co Galway, http://www.landedestates.ie.

[50]   Welsh Farmers at the Agricultural College Glasnevin, *Weekly Irish Times (1876-1941)*, 24 Sep 1910, p 12, http://proquest.umi.com/; 'Special Charter' Flight, *The Irish Times (1874-Current File)*, 27 Dec 1933, p 5, http://proquest.umi.com/; Ten Million Tons Of Coal At Slievardagh, *The Irish Times (1874-Current File)*, 8 Dec 1944, p 2; http://proquest.umi.com; http://familytreemaker.genealogy.com/users/w/o/o/Neil-F-Woodward/PDFGENEO3.pdf, viewed Mar 2009.

Anglo-Norman families from Galway City by the Cromwellians in 1652, his son, Robert 2nd Bt acquired estates in Mayo and Galway and acted as a business agent for the Clanricarde Burkes.[51]

Henry Lynch 3rd Bt was Baron of the Exchequer under James II whom he accompanied to France in 1691 after the Jacobite defeat at Aughrim. He was 'attainted of high treason' because of his commitment to James II. It has been claimed that the baronetical Lynch estate in Mayo was mainly a gift from James II. Henry's commitment to Catholicism has been emphasised by a legacy bequeathed to 'the Roman Catholic Warden and College of Galway' in his will of 1691. That commitment continued with his descendants up to Henry Lynch 5th Bt and his wife, Mary Moore, both of whom 'always were and still are Papists'. Robert Lynch 6th Bt conformed to the established church in 1750 after marriage to Elizabeth Jane Barker (heiress of Tobias Blosse, a Persian merchant) in 1749. Their descendants were required to adopt the surname, Lynch-Blosse.[52]

The branches of the Lynches in Petersburgh, Partry (otherwise Cloonlagheen) and Clogher were descended respectively from the younger sons of the 1st, 2nd and 4th baronets (Appendix 3, p 33).[53] Maurice 'Morrish', the third son of Henry Lynch 1st Bt, was transplanted by the Cromwellians to Ballynonagh (on the shores of Lough Mask, later known as Petersburgh), Clonbur, Co Galway in 1655. He also acquired land in Ballycurrin, Shrule, Co Mayo in 1679. This land, and additional land at Mount Ross Headford, Co Galway was inherited by his descendants. His great great-great grandson, the emigrant Thomas Harvey Lynch of Kansas City, disputed the inheritance of the lands of Ballycurrin to the Clerkins as willed by his second cousin, Charles Lynch, who had died without issue in 1898 (Appendix 4, p 34).[54]

He lost his case partly on the dubious grounds of being unable to provide evidence of the demise of his grandfather or his grandmother or of his grandfather's brothers and sisters. A search of the graveyard of the Lynches of Ballycurrin at Mount Ross Abbey, Headford, Co Galway failed to yield legible gravestones of his ancestors.

The 141 documents tabled at the court case included a fragment of the 1821 census of the Ballycurrin home of the 11 year old, Charles Lynch. There he lived with his parents, Peter and Julia Lynch, three brothers, three sisters, three relatives, a cook, a groom, a house maid, a kitchen maid, a laundry maid, a pantry boy, a servant and a tutor (the 21 year old, Thomas Fallon). His mother, Julia, was the granddaughter of Sir Peter Lynch of Petersburgh, Clonbur, Co Galway.

---

[51] *Burke's Peerage and Baronetage,* page 2436; Patrick Melvin, *Galway History and Society*, 1996, page 331.

[52] K W Nicholls, 'The Lynch Blosse Papers' p 146-8, 191; Lynch-Robinson, *The last of the Irish R M's*, p 23-4; Eileen O'Byrne, editor, *The convert rolls*, IMC, Dublin, 1981, p 16

[53] Patrick Melvin, *Galway History and Society*, 1996, p 331; M J Blake, 'Ballycurren Castle, Co Mayo-historical notes relating to it'; *Tuam Herald*, 17 Nov 1917, p 4.

[54] Records and genealogical papers, T.H. Lynch v M. Clarkin & others re estate of Charles Lynch (d.1897) of Ballycurrin, Co Mayo and Inchiquin Island, Lough Corrib, 1900, National Archives, Dublin, M 6179 (1-141); M J Blake, 'Ballycurren Castle, Co Mayo-Lynch of Petersburgh (Ballynonagh) and Lynch of Ballycurren', *Tuam Herald*, 24 Nov 1917, p 4; M J Blake 'Unpublished pedigrees, Lynch of Mt Ross, Headford, Lynch of Ballycurren', p 4.

Arthur, the third son of Robert Lynch 2nd Bt, settled with his mother, Ellis French, who had been assigned the estate at Partry, Ballinrobe, Co Mayo, in 1667 (Figure 13, p 13). His great grandson, Joseph Lynch (d.1785) was the father of Major Henry Blosse Lynch (1778-1823). Dr George Quested Lynch, the Kent-born son of Major Henry Blosse Lynch, returned to Partry to assist in famine relief. He died shortly afterwards of typhus fever in 1848 at the age of 35 years. His brothers, Henry (1807-72) and Thomas Ker (1818-91) became notable for their exploration of the Euphrates river route to India through the Persian Gulf as well as the Tigris river route from Baghdad to India (Database, p 87, 105, 107, 111, 119, 121). Their exploits have been commemorated by the naming of a ship 'Blosse Lynch' in their honour.[55]

In 1869, the Mayo estate of Robert Lynch-Blosse 10th Bt reportedly featured some of the most comfortable estates in the west situated on good land whose tenants had several hundred pounds in the bank. However, the bulk of the tenantry lived under impoverished and feudal conditions. Anthony Dempsey and his family of nine were scheduled for eviction on 23 November 1879 due to failure of his cash crop (oats) and his consequent inability to pay the rent. This was the first scheduled eviction since the formation of the Land League on 21 October 1879. A mass meeting was arranged featuring the anticipated attendance of Charles Stewart Parnell, leader of the Irish Parliamentary Party, and Michael Davitt, founder of the Land League. Although the eviction went ahead, the family was re-instated after payment of the rent of £26 by the Land League.[56] It appears that a new cottage was built overnight for the evicted family at the junction of three properties making it impractical to pursue a further eviction. In 1891, the estate of Robert Lynch-Blosse 10th Bt was worth £37,219 with £10,739 in Ireland. A plot had been granted to him in Balla churchyard wherein his descendants have a right to be buried there in perpetuity.[57]

In 1910, Walter Fahy of Greenhill, a tenant of Henry Lynch-Blosse 11th Bt, had his annual rent reduced from £57 to £47 arising, in part, from the demolition of six houses on his farm during the Parnell era. In 1912, Thomas Coxwell of Kilquire, West Kilmaine, Co Mayo successfully sought damages against Henry Lynch-Blosse 11th Bt arising from the alleged illegal seizure of a cow which had been purchased for £14.5.[58]

Robert Lynch-Blosse 12th Bt was effectively the last Lynch-Blosse in Co Mayo. Their estate of 18,566 acres was purchased by The Congested Districts's Board in 1909 for £154,000. Thereafter, the baronetical Lynch-Blosses settled in Britain. In 1918, the ancestral home of the Lynch-Blosses, Athavallie House in Balla, Co Mayo was converted

---

[55]   Bernard Burke, *The landed gentry of Ireland*, London, 1912, 'Lynch of Partry', p 423-4; Eilish Ellis and P Beryl Eustace, *Registry of Deeds Dublin: Abstracts of Wills, Vol III, 1785-1832*, IMC, Dublin, 1984, p 280-81; 'Partry private cemetery, Cloonlagheen, Ballyovey' *J Preservation Memorials of the Dead in Ireland*, vol 8, part 1, p 131-134; Report, Mesopotamia Commission, http://www.nationalarchives.gov.uk.

[56]   'The Port Royal Estate--Father Lavelle', *The Irish Time (1859-1874)*, 17 Aug 1869, p 3 and 'The Balla Eviction', *The Irish Times (1874-Current File)*, 22 Nov 1879, p 5, http://proquest.umi.com; 'Complaints of Ireland', *New York Times*, 23 Nov 1879, http://query.nytimes.com/mem/archive.

[57]   Lynch-Robinson, *The last of the Irish R M's*, p 23-4; 'Will of Sir Robert Lynchblosse', *The Irish Times (1874-Current File)*, 26 Feb 1894, p 5, http://proquest.umi.com; Grant of burial plot by Bishop of Tuam, Killalla and Achonry, 11 Sept 1867.

[58]   *Weekly Irish Times (1876-1941)*, 22 Oct 1910, p 4, http://proquest.umi.com; 'Novel Point Raised At Claremorris', *Weekly Irish Times (1876-1941)*, 3 Feb 1912, p 15, http://proquest.umi.com.

into a boarding school for girls run by the St Louis order (Figure 14, page 13). In 1923, the fishing rights of Sir Robert Lynch-Blosse to his former lands were reserved by deed. Richard Hely Lynch-Blosse 17th Bt (b.1953), a general practitioner in Oxfordshire, England is the current baronetical incumbent. His sister, Bridget Lynch-Blosse is an actor in Australia.[59]

Descendants of William, 2nd son of Thomas Lynch (Provost of Galway, 1274)

The descendant line of William de Lynch leads to the pedigrees of the Lynches of Antigua, Barna (Figures 15 and 16, page 14), Bordeaux, Cloghballymore (Figure 17, page 15), Drimcong, Lavally, Lydican, Lynch Grove, Montserrat and Southampton, and of Lynch Athy of Renville (Appendices 1, 2; pages 31, 32). A descendant register book for William de Lynch is comprised of 245 descendants and 121 spouses. These constitute 102 families over 22 generations to 2000 corresponding to a generational period of 32 years.

In 1784, William Hawkins, Ulster King of Arms (Chief Herald of Ireland), prepared a pedigree for Capt Isidore Lynch (then based in Paris and later Lt Gen). It indicated that he was 'lawfully descended in a direct line from Thomas Lynch of Athenry', the provost of Galway in 1274 (Appendix 2, p 32). However, the first three generations are not linked together suggesting that Hawkins was unsure of their veracity. The remaining twelve generations are linked together and are unusual in that they traverse various Lynch families including those of Athenry, Drimcong, Ballydavid, Lydican and Lynch Grove, Co Galway. Furthermore, there are differences in detail with more conventionally recorded pedigrees.[60]

As a result, the M J Blake pedigree of the Lynches of Drimcong, Moycullen, Co Galway, was difficult to integrate with that of Hawkins which recorded only two Lynches from Drimcong, namely, Thomas Lynch (3rd generation) who married Maria Athy c.1380, and Henry Lynch (12th generation) who married Helen O'Shaughnessy (living c.1700). Integration was accomplished by assuming that Thomas ? Lynch of Lydican (10th generation, the bailiff of Galway in 1595) was the father of Thomas ? Lynch of Galway whose son, Col Isidore, was allocated the house and demesne of Drimcong by the Cromwellian Commissioners in 1676.[61] This has lead to the proposition that Henry Lynch of Drimcong (12th generation, living c.1700) may be a step-nephew of Isidore, the proprietor of Drimcong (based on location and chronology). In this way, the pedigrees of Hawkins and Blake have been linked although further evidence would be desirable (Appendix 5, p 35).

Another difficulty has emerged in that John Darcy of Kiltullagh, Loughrea, Co Galway has been recorded as having married in 1752 both Elizabeth ? Lynch, daughter of

---

[59] Family: Lynch Blosse, http://www.landedestates.ie, 8 Oct 2008; Christina Murphy, 'Community buys out nuns' school', *The Irish Times (1874-Current File)*, 25 Aug, 1976, p 10, http://proquest.umi.com; Michael Viney, 'Rights In Common', *The Irish Times (1874-Current File)*, 3 Mar 1979, p 10, http://proquest.umi.com.
[60] Genealogical Office Ms 165, National Library of Ireland, p 389-392; Genealogical Office Ms 264, p 45; Genealogical Office MS 170, p 135-139; M J Blake 'An Old Lynch Manuscript' p 79-107 and 'Pedigree of Lynch of Lavally'.
[61] Martin J Blake, 'Family of Lynch of Drimcong in Moycullen Barony', *Tuam Herald*, 12 January 1929, page 4.

Thomas Lynch of Drimcong and Catherine ? Lynch, daughter of Colonel Isidore Lynch of Drimcong. It is possible that Elizabeth died shortly after her marriage in early 1752 (consistent with the fact that no children have been recorded) and that John Darcy remarried in late 1752. However, it is more probable that one of the dates is wrong. Furthermore, John Darcy of Kiltullagh has been recorded in 1752 as having married Catherine ? Lynch, daughter of Thomas Lynch of Drimcong rather than the daughter of Col Isidore Lynch of Drimcong (Appendix 6, p 36).[62] Further research is necessary.

Multiple spouses and other relatives have facilitated linkages of the descendant line of William Lynch with the pedigrees of the Lynches of Barna, Bordeaux, Lavally and Southampton, and the Lynch-Blosses of Castlecarra (Appendix 2, p 32). Most pedigrees appear to have become extinct in the male line with the exception of the Lynch-Blosses who have survived in England.

The Lynches of Bordeaux, France were established by John 'Jean' Lynch, the 12th generational descendant of William de Lynch of Galway. He was born in 1669, the son of Thomas Lynch and Margaret French of Galway. He emigrated to Bordeaux *circa* 1698 where he married Guillemette Constant in 1709. His grandson, *Jean Baptiste* Lynch (1749-1835), became Mayor of Bordeaux in 1809. After four generations in Bordeaux, the male Lynch line became extinct. Their estates are now dispersed but the name lingers on including that of Lynch-Bages, the home of the popular Michel Lynch wine.[63]

Connection of Lynch Pedigrees

Lynch pedigrees have been connected by examining the genealogy of their spouses. Such a strategy has been adopted on-line by others with varying degrees of success.[64] The spouses of the Lynches have included the following surnames: Anglo-Norman (Athy, Blake, Bodkin, Browne, Burke, French, Joyce, Martin, Skerrett); Gaelic (Crean *Ó Croidheáin*, Darcy *Ó Dorchaidhe*, Fallon, Kirwan *Ó Ciardhubháin*, O'Flaherty, O'Shaughnessy *Ó Seachnasaigh*); and English (Moore, Ormsby, Redington) (Database, p 57-149). The extent of intermarriage of the Lynches with members of these families has facilitated the connection of the various Lynch pedigrees (Table 2, next page).

The baronetical Lynches, descendants of James de Lynch, have been linked to the descendants of William de Lynch through the marriage of Eleanor, daughter of Robert Lynch 2nd Bt, to Charles O'Shaughnessy whose grandfather, Sir Roger of Gort, Co Galway was married to Ellisia Lynch. Ellisia Lynch was the great granddaughter of Joanna Penrise, the wife of Stephen Lynch, a direct descendant of William de Lynch (Appendix 5, p 35). This is but one of a number of connections between the two great pedigree lines of the Anglo-Norman Lynches of Galway, namely, the descendants of James and William, the sons of Thomas Lynch, Provost of Galway in 1274 and Bridget

[62]   Bernard Burke, 'D'arcy of Kiltulla' in *Burke's Genealogical and Heraldic History of the Landed Gentry*, London, 1847, http://books.google.ie/books; M J Blake, 'Tabular pedigrees of the D'Arcy family', *J Galway Arch Hist Soc*, 1917-1918, vol 10, p 58-66.

[63]   GO Ms 170, NLI, p 139; Bernadette Ní Loingsigh, 'Loingsigh Bhordeaux'; Michel Lynch, http://www.sparklingdirect.co.uk/wine/michel-lunch.asp, viewed 10 Mar 2009.

[64]   Camilla's genealogy (free access), http://www.links.org/; Family History (free access), http://www.peerage.com; FamilySearch (freeaccess), http://www.familysearch.org; Genealogy, the families database (fee based), http://www.stirnet.com, viewed Mar 2009.

Marshal.[65]

2. Extent of intermarriage among the dominant families in the genealogy of the Anglo-Norman Lynches whose ancestors settled in Galway
(as downloaded from the author's BrothersKeeper.com database on 17 March 2009).

Surname	Male	Female	Total	Approx fraction of marriages to Lynch
Athy	15	12	27	1 in 4 (4/15)
Blake	104	43	147	1 in 2 (34/72)
Bodkin	21	12	33	1 in 2.5 (8/20)
Browne	38	35	73	1 in 2 (25/51)
Burke	50	39	89	1 in 5 (12/64)
Darcy	32	12	44	1 in 5 (7/35)
French	30	29	59	1 in 2 (20/46)
Joyce	13	11	24	1 in 2 (10/17)
Kirwan	11	11	22	1 in 3 (6/18)
Lynch	481	289	770	1 in 8 (45/345)
Lynch-Blosse	20	11	31	Zero/19
Lynch-Staunton	10	8	18	Zero/8
Martin	34	24	58	1 in 5 (7/38)
Skerrett	9	8	17	1 in 2 (6/13)
Totals	868	544	1412	1 in 4 (184/761)

The connection of the Lynches of Renville, Oranmore, Co Galway to the Athys and Lynch Athys is difficult to unravel as the sources are in conflict. The connection commenced with the marriage of Maria, daughter of Philip Lynch of Galway and Renville, to John Ormsby of Cloghballymore (Appendix 7, p 37). Their grandnephew, Philip Lynch, bequeathed the Renville estate to his nephew, Philip Athy, on condition that he assumed the surname of Lynch. However, it has also been claimed that Philip Lynch, bequeathed the Renville estate to his daughter, Margaret, in clear conflict with the provisions of his 1716 will in which no children are recorded; rather, Margaret is recorded as his sister. It appears that the will is correct and the other sources are in error. The only remaining difficulty is the annotation of John Ormsby of Dublin as the uncle of Philip Lynch, which would be true if he were the brother of Oliver Ormsby and the son of his father, John Ormsby of Galway.[66]

The Lynches of Lowberry, Co Roscommon have been linked to the Lynches of Barna, Cloghballymore and Hollybrook (Appendix 6, p 36). It was assumed that Francis

---

[65]   M J Blake, 'O'Shaughnessy of Gort (1543-1783): Tabular Pedigree' *J Galway Arch Hist Soc*, 1909-10, vol 6, p 58-64; M J Blake, 'O'Shaughnessy Tabular Pedigree-Correction' *JGAHS*, 1911-12, vol 7, p 53; M J Blake 'An Old Lynch Manuscript', p 96.

[66]   Pedigree of Lynch of Renville, Co Galway, *c.*1600-*c.*1720, GO Ms 161, NLI, p 102, 107; Will of Philip Lynch of Renville, 1716, in P Beryl Eustace, *Registry of Deeds Dublin: Abstracts of Wills, Vol I, 1708-1745*, IMC, Dublin, 1956, p 54; Burke, *The landed gentry of Ireland*, 'Athy of Renville', p 15, 16.

Lynch who married Julia, eldest daughter of Maurice Blake of Ballinafad, Co Mayo was the same Francis Lynch of Lowberry who married the unnamed daughter of Maurice Blake of Ballinafad. The Lynches of Lowberry are also linked to the Crean-Lynches through the marriage of a Lynch of Lowberry (assumed to be Julie, daughter of Francis Lynch) to Dominick Crean-Lynch.[67]

The pedigrees of the baronet Brownes of the Neale, Ballinrobe, Co Mayo and the Burkes of Castlehackett and Ower, Co Galway have enabled the integration of the pedigrees of the Lynches of Dughisky (Merlinpark), Co Galway and the Crean Lynches of Clogher and Hollybrook, Co Mayo. The Lynches of Shrule (Figure 18, p 15) also connect with the Redingtons of Kilcornan who connect with the Wilson Lynches (Figure 19, p 15) of Renmore and Durus. The proposed connection of the Redingtons of Kilcornan with the Lynches of Lydican and Argentina has not been supported by documentary evidence.[68]

The four-generation pedigree of the family of Alderman Anthony Lynch of Galway who died in 1638 has been recorded (Figure 5, p 8). He may be the 'Anthonie Linch, alderman' who signed a petition requesting the retention of Capt Henry Clare as commander of HM forces in Galway city. His daughter, Garret Lynch, married Dominick Darcy of Galway who was transplanted to Clonuane, Co Clare in 1656. Dominick was the grandson of James 'Rivagh' Darcy (d.1603) whose second wife, Elizabeth Martin, later married Henry Lynch 1st Bt (d.1634) thus linking the two great Lynch pedigree lines.[69]

Lynches connected to famous people and events

The marital strategy also facilitated a linkage of the Lynches with famous people and events including the Bodkin massacre, Che Guevara, James II, Richard 'Humanity Dick' Martin MP, Grace O'Malley, Patrick Sarsfield and Bram Stoker.

The linkage with the Bodkin massacre commenced with Marie, the daughter of Captain Stephen Lynch, of Berwick's regiment in France. She married Oliver Bodkin of Carrowbane, Tuam, Co Galway who was brutally murdered along with nine or ten others in 1741 by three conspirators including his older son, John Bodkin, and his step-brother, Dominick 'Blind' Bodkin. Among those murdered was Marcus Lynch, a Galway merchant, who may have been a relative of Marie Lynch who had passed away in 1730.[70]

---

[67]   Genealogical Office Ms 264, NLI, p 48; Pedigree of Lynch of Dughisky (Merlin Park), Co Galway and Lynch/Crean Lynch and Lynch of Gahody, *c.*1720-*c.*1800, in National Library of Ireland Ms 112, p 328 (Burke), p 329 (Browne).

[68]   GO Ms 112, NLI, p 328 (Burke), p 329 (Browne); Draft pedigree of Linch of Lydican, Co Galway and Buenos Aires, c 1670-c 1750, NLI, Ms 817, p 12; Brian McGinn, 'Che Guevara's Irish blood.'

[69]   Ms 264, NLI, p 50; Petition on Behalf of Capt Henry Clare, Calendar of the Manuscripts of the Marquis of Salisbury, vol 12, 1602, no 172, 1910, State Papers Online, Part 1 http://go.galegroup.com/mss/basicSearch, 2008; M J Blake, 'Tabular pedigrees of the D'Arcy family'.

[70]   Priscilla O'Connor 'Irish clerics and Jacobites in early eighteenth-century Paris, 1700-30' in *The Irish in Europe, 1580-1815*, Thomas O'Connor, editor, Dublin, 2001, p 186; John Bodkin, Dominick Bodkin and others-Executed in Ireland on 26th of March, 1742, for the Murder of Eleven Persons, The Newgate Calendar Part II (1742 to 1799), http://www.exclassics.com/newgate/newgate2.txt; Oliver J. Burke, *Anecdotes of the Connaught Circuit, from its foundation in 1604*, Dublin, 1885, p 86-92; Jarlath O'Connell, *The Bodkin murders*, http://places.galwaylibrary.ie, viewed Jan 2009.

The Lynch connection with the Bodkins of Carrowbaun and Carrowbeg was re-established when Hyacinth, the great grandnephew of Oliver Bodkin married Bell, daughter of John Lynch of Bellwell (probably Belwell, Dunmore, Co Galway). No connection was found with Edmond Bodkin of Kilcloony, Co Galway whose niece, Mabella Lynch, was the daughter of his sister, Elinor.[71]

The Lynches of Argentina have been linked to Patrick 'Patricio' Lynch who was born in Galway in 1715, the son of Patrick Lynch and Agnes Blake, the grandson of William Lynch and Catherine Blake and the great grandson of Michael Lynch and Mary Browne.[72] He emigrated to Argentina via Spain. His great great-grand-daughter was Ana Lynch y Ortiz (1861-1947) who was a grandmother of the revolutionary, Ernesto Che Guevara (1928-1967).

The legendary Grace O'Malley of Clare Island, Co Mayo may be linked to the Lynch-Blosse family of Castlecarra, Ballinrobe, Co Mayo through the pedigrees of both her first and second husbands. The pedigree of her first husband, *Donal-an-Chogaidh* O'Flaherty, does not appear to be reliable as he has been incorrectly entered as Timothy 'Teig' O'Flaherty, 2nd husband. This is but one of a number of errors in an on-line O'Flaherty pedigree. Linkage through her second husband, Sir Richard-in-Iron Bourke (so-called for his habit of wearing a suit of armour) is easier to establish as their great great-granddaughter, Margaret, married Henry Lynch 3rd Bt of Castlecarra. Margaret was also the grandaunt of Joan, the daughter of Theobold Bourke 6th Vt. Joan Bourke married Murrough, father of Sir John O'Flaherty of Lemonfield, Oughterard thus providing a possible linkage to the O'Flaherty line.[73]

The claim to fame of Richard 'Humanity Dick' Martin MP (1754-1834) of Ballinahinch, Connemara resides primarily in his commitment to animal rights, which was a seminal influence in the formation of the Society for the Prevention of Cruelty to Animals in 1824. His general benevolence led to the formation of his nickname 'Humanity Dick' prompted by the Prince Regent, later George IV. In 1777, he married the beautiful and talented Elizabeth, daughter of George Vesey of Hollymount, Co Mayo and the step-niece of Elizabeth Lynch.[74] However, Elizabeth Vesey had an affair with the Irish rebel, Theobald Wolfe Tone, who had tutored Martin's half-brothers in Ballinahinch. She later eloped with George Petrie to London. At an earlier stage, Robert Martin of Dangan, Connemara, the father of 'Humanity Dick' married Elizabeth, daughter of Oliver Lynch, a descendant of the Lynches of Barna, Co Galway (Appendix 8, p 38). Robert was the great great-great-great-grandson of Richard Martin, Mayor of Galway (1607, 1611, 1621) whose daughter Elizabeth, married Henry Lynch, 1st Bt, of Corrandulla, Co Galway.

[71] Land holdings, Genealogical Office Ms 32484, National Library of Ireland; Will 408, Edmond Bodkin, Kilcloony, Co Galway, 1767 in P Beryl Eustace, *Registry of Deeds Dublin: Abstracts of Wills, Vol II, 1746-85*, page 201.
[72] Brian McGinn, 'Che Guevara's Irish blood.'
[73] Grace O' Malley, http://www.links.org/links-cgi/readged?/home/ben/camilla-genealogy/current+c-omalley, viewed Jan 2009; Anne Chambers, *Granuaile (Grace O'Malley): Ireland's Pirate Queen c. 1530-1603*, Dublin, 2003, page 179.
[74] Shevawn Lynam, *Humanity Dick 'King of Connemara' 1754-1834*, Dublin, 1989, p 300; Richard Martin, (Galway) Ireland, b. 1754, http://www.familysearch.org.

Patrick Sarsfield, first Earl of Lucan, married Anne, the daughter of Rory O'Moore who was reportedly involved in the Irish Rebellion of 1641. Patrick Sarsfield joined forces with James II during the Jacobite war; he is remembered for his leadership in the defence of Limerick in 1690 against the forces of William of Orange. In the following year, he married Honora, daughter of William Bourke, 7th Earl of Clanricarde. Honora Bourke later married (1695) James fitz James, 1st Duke of Berwick-Upon-Tweed, the illegitimate son of James II and Arabella Churchill. Arabella was the daughter of Sir Winston Churchill, MP of England. The linkage of Patrick Sarsfield to the Lynches arises from the subsequent marriage in 1853 of Robert Lynch-Blosse 10th Bt to Harriet, the daughter of Howe Peter Browne, 2nd Marquess of Sligo and Hester Catherine de Burgh. Hester Catherine was the daughter of General John Thomas de Burgh, 13th Earl of Clanricarde. The General was the great great-grandson of William Bourke 7th Earl of Clanricarde, the father of Honora who had married Patrick Sarsfield in 1691 (Appendix 9, p 39). Patrick Sarsfield was also a cousin of Robert Martin of Dangan, Galway (the father of Richard 'Humanity Dick' Martin MP) who by 1747 was reportedly head of the Connaught Jacobites. It may also be of interest to note that Henry Lynch 3rd Bt was a close associate of James II and accompanied him to France after his defeat at Aughrim, Co Galway in 1691.[75]

The Lynches of Garracloon, Co Mayo have been connected with Bram Stoker, the author of *Dracula*. His mother, Charlotte Mathilda Blake Thornley, was the niece of General George Blake who was executed in 1798. George Blake was the great grandson of Mark Lynch and Anne Lynch both of Garracloon. Thus, Anne Lynch was the great great-great-grandmother of Bram Stoker (Appendix 10, p 40). She appears to have been confused with Anne Lynch, the grandmother of George Moore (1852-1933).[76]

Conclusion

The pedigrees of the Anglo-Norman Lynches who settled in Galway after the Anglo-Norman invasion of Ireland in 1169 have been mostly derived from the descendants of James and William, the sons of Thomas Lynch, Provost of Galway in 1274. The pedigrees accompanied by the relevant documentary sources have been entered onto a BrothersKeeper.com database, an extract of which is included (Database, pages 57-149). Those pedigrees, which have been interconnected, include the Lynches of Ballycurrin and Petersburg, Barna, Drimcong, Lavally, Partry, Renmore and Duras, and Shrule; and of Lynch Athy, Lynch-Blosse and Crean-Lynch.

Most pedigrees appear to have become extinct in the male line tending to coincide with the decline of the landed gentry in Ireland towards the end of the 19th century. However, recorded pedigrees normally focus on the surviving eldest sons to whom

---

[75] John Todhunter, *Life of Patrick Sarsfield*, London, 1895; Lady Honora Bourke, http://www.thepeerage.com/p10598.htm#i105979, viewed Apr 2009; Adrian J Martyn, 'The Martin-Eyre Feud, 1652-1748, Part 1', *Galway Advertiser*, 27 July 2000, p 30, http://www.martinhistory.net/27_July_OldGalway.pdf, May 2008.

[76] Murray, *A life of Bram Stoker*, p 8 and 9; Will 64, Mark Lynch, Garracloon, Co Mayo, 1749 in P Beryl Eustace, *Registry of Deeds Dublin: Abstracts of Wills, Vol II, 1746-85*, p 32, 33; J.H. Montgomery & Son, includes wills of Mark Lynch of Garracloon 1750 & Martin Blake Lynch of Dublin 1801, Small Accs Index 88, National Archives; M J, Blake, 'A transplanter's decree of Final Settlement by the Loughrea Commissioners in Cromwell's time', *J Galway Arch Hist Soc*, 1903-1904, vol 3, p 148-153.

property was generally bequeathed. Thus, many members of the Lynch families were not recorded in the pedigrees. Furthermore, the Lynch line in Ireland was probably supplemented through children born out of wedlock. Peter, the apparently disabled or illiterate brother of Robert Lynch 6th Bt, died without lawful issue but was father to seven sons and five daughters to each of whom he bequeathed £500.[77] In similar fashion, his nephew, Henry Lynch-Blosse 7th Bt, bequeathed £18,800 to his seven children born out of wedlock by his mistress, Sibella Cottle, although his will may have been challenged by members of his family. The Lynch line in Ireland is further complicated by the Lynches of Gaelic origin, *Ó Loinsigh*, who are now virtually indistinguishable from the Anglo-Norman Lynches.

Lynch pedigrees, not yet interconnected, have also been entered onto the database and include: a 13 generation pedigree of Stanislaus Lynch of Galway (93 people); the Lynches of Lydican and Argentina (36 people); the Lynches of Garracloon, Co Mayo (33 people); the three-generation pedigree of the family of Nicholas fitz Francis Lynch of Galway based on his will of 1740-41 (12 people); Joseph Lynch of Ballyovey, Partry, Co Mayo (11 people); and some smaller groups.[78]

Scrutiny of the records of births, marriages and deaths for the parishes of St Nicholas South and West Galway, and St Nicholas North and East Galway ranging from 1690 to 1868 may help to enhance pedigree connectivity. For example, Cecilia French, a witness at the baptism of John Patrick, son of Robert Lynch and Maria Morris in 1690 could be the same woman who married Bryan Oge O'Flaherty in 1707. If so, an additional pedigree linkage might be established between the O'Flahertys and the Lynches as Bryan Oge O'Flaherty is a cousin of Bibyan O'Flaherty. Bibyan married Peter, the son of Robuck Lynch 2nd Bt (d.1677) and Ellis French.[79]

The will of Mark Lynch of Garracloon, Cong, Co Mayo has been included among the documents surrounding the partition of lands in Co Galway between his grandson, Martin Blake Lynch of Dublin and Mark Browne Lynch of Newtown, Co Galway. The Lynches of Garracloon may be connected to the Lynches of Lowberry because Thomas Lynch of Lowberry married the daughter of Martin Browne of Cloonfad, Co Roscommon in 1782, and John Browne Lynch of Lowberry (son of Thomas?) married Ms Browne of Cloonkeely, Co Galway.[80]

The origin (Anglo-Norman or Gaelic) of the author's relatives, the Lynches of Bodane, Tuam, Co Galway (from whom Cardinal Terence Cooke of New York, 1921-1983 is descended) is not yet established. The Lynches of Bodane may be related to

---

[77] K W Nicholls, 'The Lynch Blosse Papers', Prerogative Will of Peter Lynch, 1810, p 154-5.

[78] M J Blake 'Some former Lynch families of Co Galway-pedigrees hitherto unpublished-ancestry of Stanislaus Lynch and his relations'; O'Byrne and Chamney *The convert rolls, 1703-1838*, p 384; Will 438, Joseph Lynch of Cloonlagheen, Ballyovey (Partry), Co Mayo, 1813, in Ellis and Eustace, *Registry of Deeds Dublin: Abstracts of Wills, Vol III, 1785-1832*, p 280-1.

[79] Parishes of St Nicholas S and W Galway, and St Nicholas N and E Galway, Microfilms P 2436-7, NLI; http://www.links.org/links-cgi/rcadged?/home/ben/camilla-genealogy, viewed May 2009.

[80] Guinness, Mahon Collection, includes deed of partition of lands in county of the town of Galway & Co Galway & map, Martin Blake Lynch of Dublin & Mark Browne Lynch of Newtown, Co Galway, 16 Aug 1777, Small Accs Index 59, D 5784-5786 & CO 1075-1076, National Archives; J.H. Montgomery & Son, includes wills of Mark Lynch of Garracloon 1750 & Martin Blake Lynch of Dublin 1801; Browne (Cloonfad), Browne (Moyne), http://www.landedestates.ie, viewed Apr 2009.

the Lynches of Ballycurrin due to the proximity of their land to the Lynch land in Bodane, Kilconly, Co Galway. Scrutiny of the gravestones in Ross Abbey, Headford, Co Galway where some of the Lynches of Ballycurrin are buried may is unlikely to be helpful as the inscriptions are probably illegible.[81]

Unconnected individuals entered onto the database include some Church of Ireland Lynches whose baptisms and marriages have been recorded. Both the Protestant bishop of Kilmacduagh and Clonfert (1587-1625), Roland Lynch and the Catholic Archbishop of Tuam (1669-1713), James Lynch have been entered onto the database in the hope that their genealogy may be established. In contrast, Thomas Lynch, the second youngest signatory of the American Declaration of Independence in 1776, has not been entered onto the database as he may have been a descendant of the Gaelic Lynches of Cork.[82]

Further research is required to address these and other challenges including the early genealogy of the Lynches. The latter requires further study to resolve (where possible) some of the conflicting evidence in the various manuscript pedigrees. The BrothersKeeper.com database also requires further development to make it more user-friendly and informative. In that context, a PDF representation of the 1726 connected individuals (or subsets thereof) of the Anglo-Norman Lynches who settled in Galway would be useful. It could be similar to Neil F Woodward's PDF file which included 21 generations of the Lynch-Blosse family and their Lynch ancestors.[83]

Acknowledgement

The author wishes to gratefully acknowledge: the pioneering work of Martin J Blake (1853-1931), Member of the Royal Irish Academy, in recording the pedigrees of the landed gentry of the counties of Galway and Mayo; Sean Murphy MA for expert guidance in genealogical methodology; Richard Hely Lynch-Blosse, 17th Bt, Oxfordshire who supplied scans of photographs, letters and portraits of some members of the extended Lynch-Blosse family as well as supplementary family information; Marie McFeely, National Gallery of Ireland, who identified the portrait of Mrs Kelly of the Lynches of Barna; Bridget Lynch-Blosse of Australia who introduced the author to Craig Lynch-Blosse of New Zealand from whom I received images of his great grandparents, Edward and Edith Lynch-Blosse, and through whom I discovered Neil F Woodward's pdf file which included an on-line pedigree of the Lynch-Blosse family.

---

[81] Gerarda McHugh, 'Lynch's Mill at Bodane'; Records and genealogical papers re T.H. Lynch v M. Clarkin re estate of Charles Lynch of Ballycurrin, Co Mayo 1900.

[82] Brigid Clesham, *The register of the parish of St Nicholas, (Church of Ireland) Galway, 1792-1840*, 163 p; *Burke's landed gentry*, 1912, 'Lynch of Duras', p 423; Aoife Williams, *Lynch: This is the History of your Surname*, Ennis, Ireland.

[83] Lynch-Blosse pedigree in familytreemaker.genealogy.com/users/w/o/o/Neil-F-Woodward/PDFGENEO3.pdf, viewed Apr 2009.

Appendix 1: Proposed pedigree of the Anglo-Norman Lynches who settled in Galway commencing with the Anglo-Norman invasion of Ireland in 1169.[84]

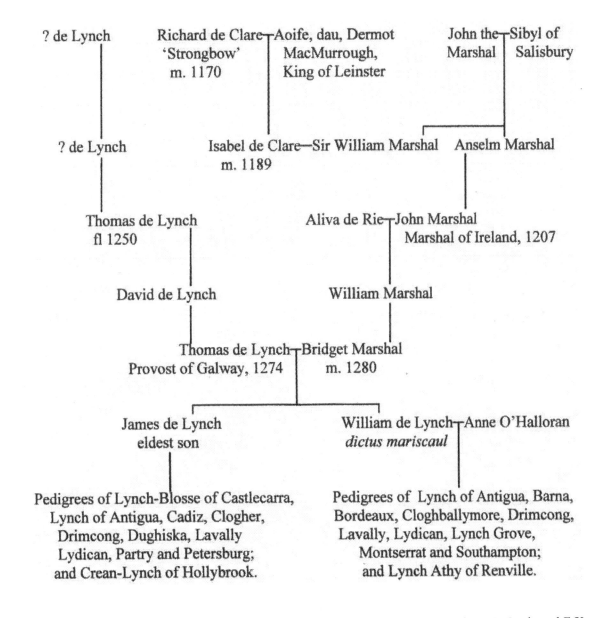

Sources: Ms 165, p 389, Ms 170, p 135, Ms 264, p 45, National Library of Ireland; T W Moody and F X Martin, *The course of Irish history*, p 95-112; H. S Sweetman, *Calendar of documents, relating to Ireland*, 1171-1307; M J Blake, *JGAHS*, vol 8, 1913-14, p 81, 82, 85, 86; vol 9, 1915-16, p 79; and vol 10, 1917-18, p 66-69; William Playfair, *British Family Antiquity*, p 51-54; Catherine Armstrong 'William Marshal-Earl of Pembroke' http://www.castlewales.com/marshall.html , viewed Apr 2009.

---

[84]   Playfair contends that William *le Petite* is the common ancestor of all the Lynches of Ireland: William *le Petite* father of Nicholas f. John f. Maurice f. Hugh f. David f. Thomas f. James f. Thomas f. David Lynch f. Thomas m. Bridget Marshal, 1280. The timing is problematic as it is not possible to fit 10 generations between the arrival of the Anglo-Normans in Ireland in 1169 and the marriage of Thomas in 1280.

Appendix 2: Pedigree of William, 2nd son of Thomas Lynch (Provost of Galway, 1274), including the pedigree of Isidore Lynch and linkages to the pedigrees of the Lynches of Barna, Bordeaux, Lavally and Southampton.

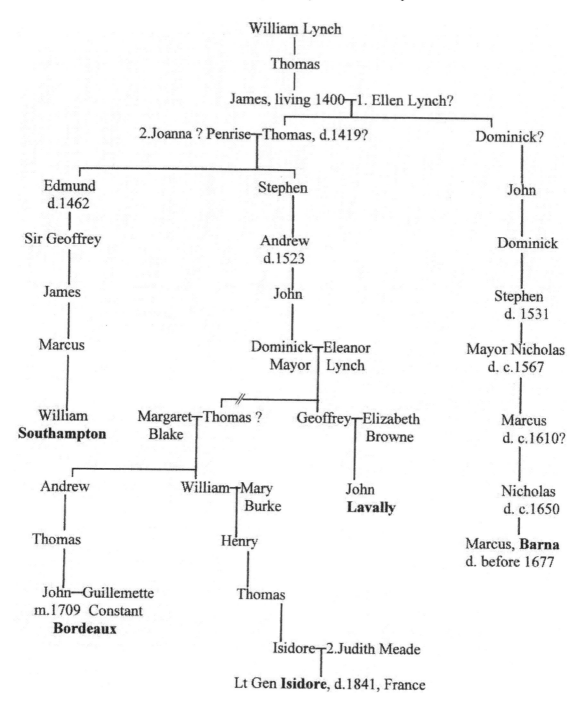

Sources: Lynch of Galway, Betham, NLI, Ms 264, p 45-50; Pedigree of Lynch of Castlecarra, Clogher, Co Mayo and of Cadiz in Spain, 1250-c 1812, NLI, Ms 170, p 135-139; Pedigree of Lynch of Athenry, Drimcong, Ballydavid, Lydican and Lynch's Grove, and of Paris, *c* 1430-1784, NLI, MS 165, p 389-392; M J Blake 'An Old Lynch Manuscript' *JGAHS* 9, 79-107 and 'Pedigree of Lynch of Lavally' 10, 66-9.

Appendix 3: Pedigree of James, son of Thomas Lynch (Provost of Galway, 1274),
including a partial pedigree of the Lynch-Blosses of Castlecarra, and linkages to the
pedigrees of the Lynches of Ballynonagh, Clogher, Drimcong, Dughiska, Lavally, Partry
and Petersburg in the counties of Galway and Mayo.

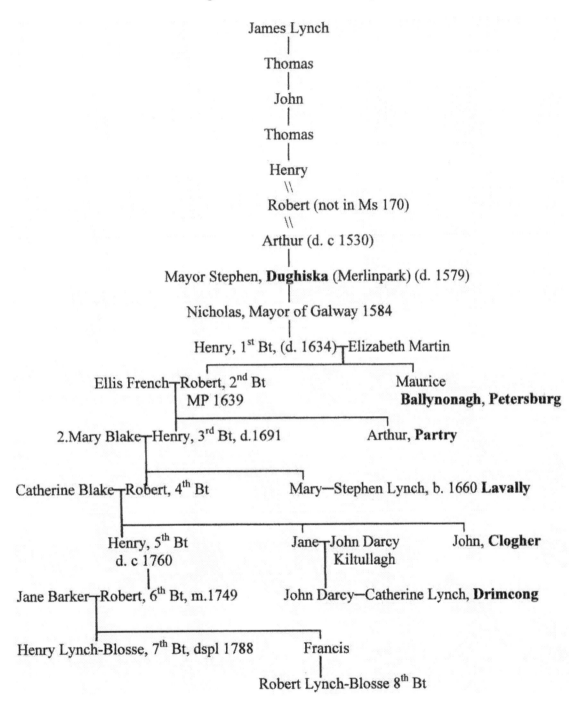

Sources: Lynch of Galway, Betham, NLI, Ms 264, p 45-50; Pedigree of Lynch of Castlecarra, Clogher, Co
Mayo and of Cadiz in Spain, 1250-*c* 1812, NLI, MS 170, p 135-139; James Hardiman, *The History of the
Town of Galway*; Patrick Melvin, 'Galway Tribes as Landowners and Gentry,' *Galway History and Society*.

Appendix 4: Pedigree of the Lynches of Ballynonagh, Petersburg, Co Galway and of
Ballycurrin, Shrule, Co Mayo as related to the case of the emigrant Thomas Harvey
Lynch of Kansas City who disputed the inheritance of the lands of Ballycurrin by the
Clerkins as willed by his second cousin, Charles Lynch.

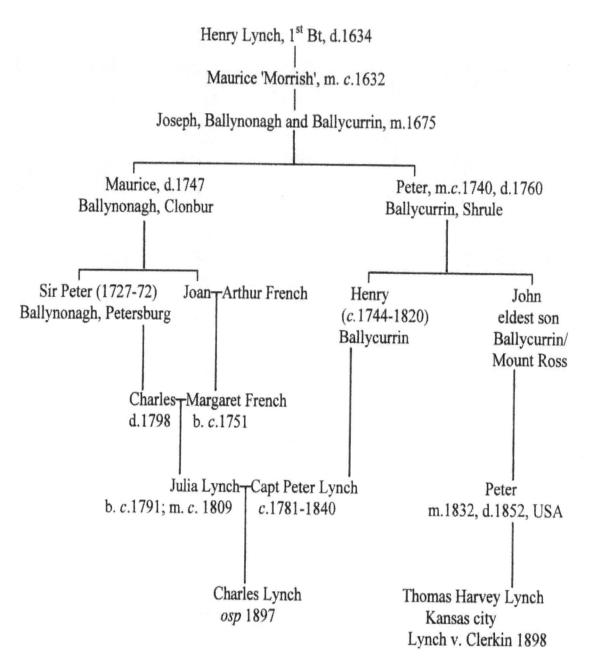

Sources: Records and genealogical papers re case of T.H. Lynch v M. Clarkin re estate of Charles Lynch
(d.1897) of Ballycurrin, Co Mayo, 1900, National Archives; M J Blake, 'Ballycurren Castle, Co Mayo-
families of Lynch of Petersburgh (Ballynonagh) and Lynch of Ballycurren,' *Tuam Herald*, 24 Nov 1917, 5
Jan 1929, pages 4; M J Blake 'Unpublished pedigrees of Lynch families-Lynch of Mount Ross, Headford
and Lynch of Ballycurren', *Tuam Herald*, 22, 29 Dec 1928, pages 4.

Appendix 5: Proposed descendants of Stephen Lynch of Lydican, Claregalway,
Co Galway by his wives, Joanna Penrise and Margaret Athy.

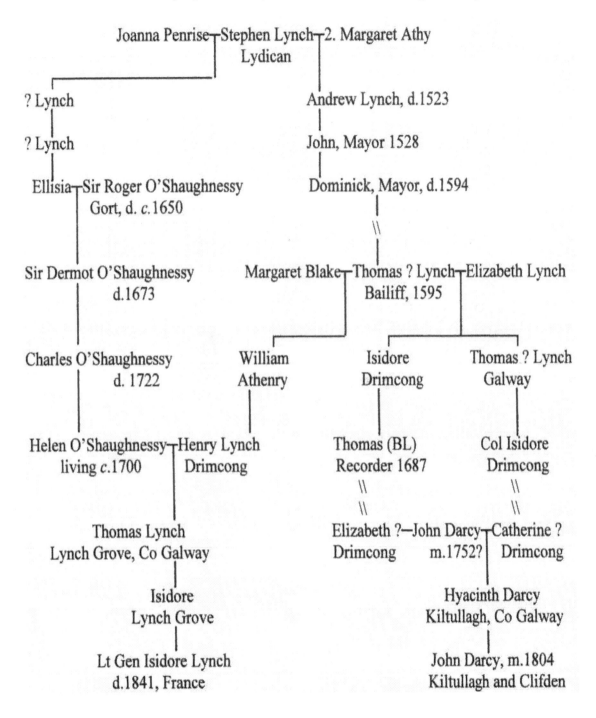

Sources: Ms 165 p 389-392, Ms 264 p 45 and Ms 170 p 135-139, NLI; M J Blake 'An Old Lynch Manuscript,' *JGAHS*, vol 9, 1915-16, p 79-107, 'Tabular pedigrees of the D'Arcy family', 1917-1918, vol 10, p 58-66 and 'Pedigree of Lynch of Lavally,' vol 10, p 66-69; M J Blake, 'Family of Lynch of Drimcong in Moycullen Barony.' *Tuam Herald*, 12 Jan 1929, p 4; 'D'arcy of Kiltulla', *Burke's Landed Gentry*.

Appendix 6: Connection of various Anglo-Norman Lynch families by marriage with the
Anglo-Norman Blakes of Ballinafad, Castlebar, Co Mayo;
the Gaelic Creans of Hollybrook, Claremorris, Co Mayo;
the Gaelic Darcys of Kiltullagh, Loughrea, Co Galway;
and the Anglo-Norman Frenches of Durus, Kinvara, Co Galway.

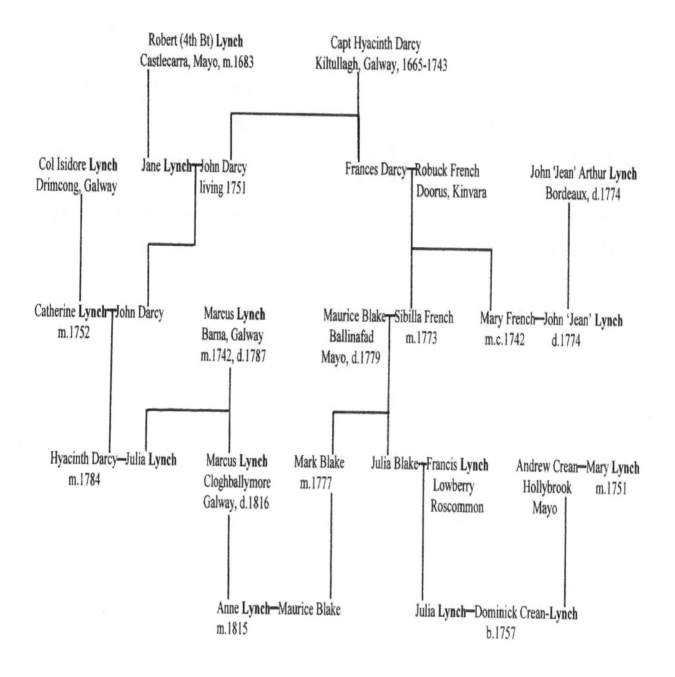

Sources: Ms 112, Ms 170, Ms 180, Ms 264, National Library of Ireland; *Burke's landed gentry*, 1965;
Blake04, Darcy05, http://www.stirnet.com, viewed Mar 2009.

Appendix 7: Pedigree of Lynch and Lynch Athy of Renville, Oranmore, Co Galway (forenames in bold are those cited in the 1716 will of Philip Lynch of Renville).[85]

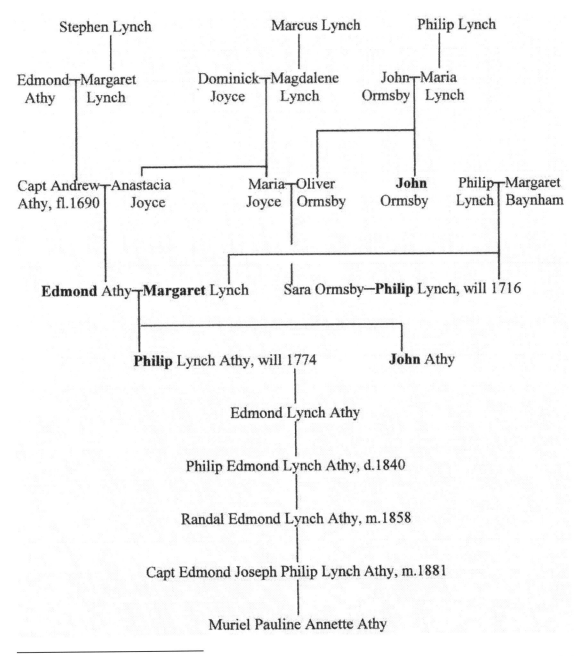

[85]   Pedigree of Lynch of Renville, *c.*1600-*c.*1720, NLI, Ms 161, p 107, 102; Burke, *The landed gentry of Ireland*, 1912, 'Athy of Renville', p 15, 16; Lynch, Philip, re Renville estate to (uncle) John Ormsby of Dublin, Registry of Deeds; Will of Philip Lynch of Renville, 1716 in Eustace, *Registry of Deeds Dublin: Abstracts of Wills, Vol I, 1708-1745*, p 54 ; Seathrún of Dubhros, 'The Killykellys of Cloghballymore.'

Appendix 8: Marital connections of the Anglo-Norman Lynches of Barna and Corrundulla, County Galway and of Castlecarra, County Mayo with the Martins of Connemara and Tullira, County Galway.

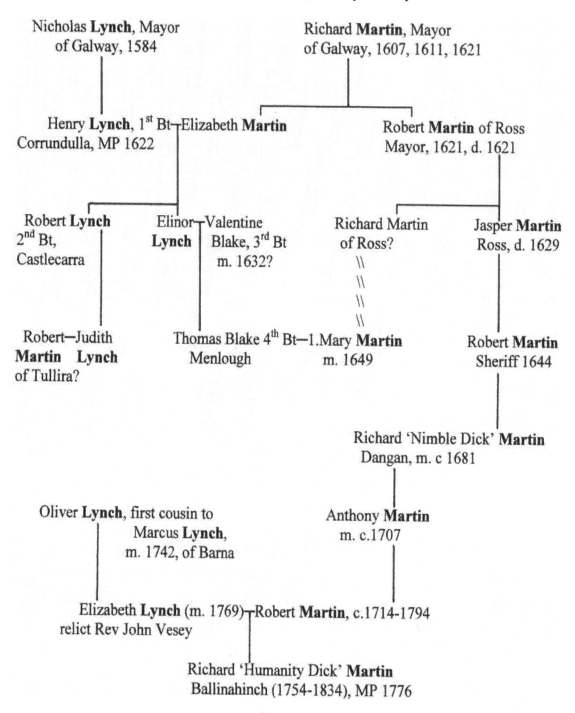

Sources: *Burke's Landed Gentry*, 1912, 'Blake of Tower Hill'; 'Martin of Ross'; *Burke's Peerage and Baronetage*, 2003, 'Lynch-Blosse'; Hardiman 'The History of Galway', p 212, 213; Lynam, *Humanity Dick 'King of Connemara' 1754-1834*; Mary Martin, http://www.thepeerage.com/p14379.htm#i143783; Richard Martin, http://www.familysearch.org/, viewed Apr 2009.

The genealogy of the Anglo-Norman Lynches who settled in Galway

Appendix 9: Relationship of Robert Lynch-Blosse, 10th Bt (1825-1893) to
Patrick Sarsfield (d. *circa* 1693) and to James II (1633-1701)
via the Westport Brownes and the Clanricarde Burkes.

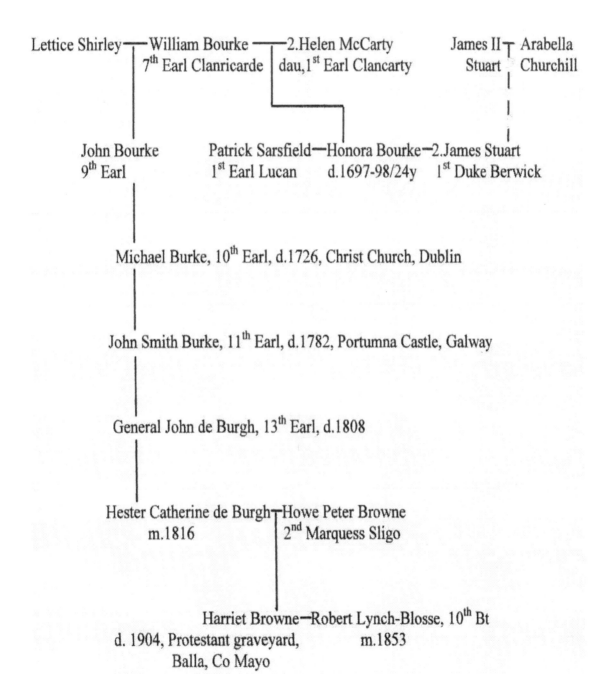

Sources: Lady Honora Bourke, http://www.thepeerage.com; *Burke's Peerage and Baronetage*, 2003,
Lynch-Blosse, p 2436; William III of England, http://en.wikipedia.org, viewed 3 Dec 2008.

Appendix 10: The Anglo-Norman Lynch and Blake ancestors of
Abraham 'Bram' Stoker (1847-1912), the author of *Dracula* as presented in a
descendant register book from the author's database on BrothersKeeper.com

Generation One

1. **William Lynch** of Galway.
> *Children:*
> + 2   i.   Andrew Lynch.

Generation Two

2. **Andrew Lynch** of Galway and Garracloon, Cong, Ballinrobe, Co Mayo, d. 3 May
1664. Allocated lands of Garracloon, 1657, by Cromwellian Commissioners at
Loughrea.
> *Children:*
> 3   i.   John Lynch, b. in Garracloon, Mayo, Ireland, d. 14 Feb 1678.
> + 4   ii.   Marcus Lynch.

Generation Three

4. **Marcus Lynch**, b. in Garracloon, d. 14 July 1725. Married 28 July 1679, Mary
French.
> *Children:*
> + 5   i.   Anne Lynch.

Generation Four

5. **Anne Lynch**, b. in Garracloon, d. 22 Nov 1744. Married 16 June 1707, Mark Lynch
of Garracloon (son of James Lynch); d. 23 Sep 1749; Will, 31 March 1750,
Prerogative Court.
> *Children:*
> + 6   i.   Julia 'Juliane' Lynch.
> 7   ii.   Mary Lynch, married Thomas Browne of Newtown, Abbeyknockmoy.

Generation Five

6. **Julia 'Juliane' Lynch**, b. in Garracloon, d. c.1790; Will, PC, 1790. Married 18 Apr
1728, George Blake; b. July 1700 of Killernane, Ballinrobe (son of Martin Blake); d.
11 Sept 1771; Will, 19 Oct 1769, PC; buried Ross Abbey.
> *Children:*
> 8   i.   Martin (BL) Blake Lynch, b. 3 Oct 1731, d. c.1799 dsp; Will, 19 July
>   1799, PC. He married Julia 'Juliane' Kirwan.
> + 9   ii.   Marcus 'Mark' Blake.
> + 10   iii.   Richard Blake b. 31 May 1736.

Appendix 10 (continued) The Anglo-Norman Lynch and Blake ancestors of Abraham 'Bram' Stoker (1847-1912), the author of *Dracula* as presented in a descendant register book from the author's database on BrothersKeeper.com.[86]

Generation Six

9. **Marcus 'Mark' Blake**, married Mary O'Donnell (daughter of Col Manus O'Donnell).
    Children:
    11   i.   Marcus 'Mark' Blake, eldest son.

10. **Richard Blake**, b. 31 May 1736 in Garracloon, d. 1801; Will, 2 Aug 1799, PC. He married Eliza O'Donnell, b. in of Newport, Mayo (daughter of Col Manus O'Donnell).
    Children:
    12   i.   George (General) Blake, d. 8 Sep 1798, executed Ballinamuck, Longford.
    + 13   ii.   Matilda Blake.

Generation Seven

13. **Matilda Blake**, m. 3 Oct 1817 in Ballyshannon, Donegal, Capt Thomas Thornley.
    Children:
    + 14   i.   Charlotte M Blake Thornley, b. 28 June 1818.
    15   ii.   Thomas Blake Thornley, b. 1822, d. 1850.

Generation Eight

14. **Charlotte M Blake Thornley**, b. 28 June 1818, d. 1901; married 1844, Abraham Stoker; b. 1799, d. 10 October 1876.
    Children:
    16   i.   Abraham 'Bram' Stoker, b. 8 Nov 1847 in 15 Marino Crescent, Clontarf, Dublin, d. 20 Apr 1912; m. 1878, Florence Balcombe; b. 1858, d. 1937.

---

[86]   M J Blake, 'A transplanter's decree of Final Settlement by the Loughrea Commissioners in Cromwell's time.' 1903-1904, vol 3, p 153; M J Blake, *Blake family records, 1600-1700*, p 196-200; J.H. Montgomery & Son, solicitor's collection, includes wills of Mark Lynch of Garracloon 1750 & Martin Blake Lynch of Dublin 1801 re the partition of lands in 1777, Small Accs. Index 88, National Archives; Murray, *From the shadow of Dracula: A life of Bram Stoker*, p 8; Belford, *Bram Stoker: A biography of the author of Dracula*, 1996, p 21; Lynch (Garracloon), Blake (Garracloon), http://www.landedestates.ie, Apr 2009.

Primary Sources

National Library of Ireland
Births, marriages and deaths, parishes of St Nicholas S and W Galway, and St Nicholas N and E Galway, 1690-1868, Microfilms P 2436-37.
Draft pedigree of Linch of Lydican, Co Galway and Buenos Aires, *c*.1670-*c*.1750, Genealogical Office Ms 817, page 12.
Land holdings, Genealogical Office Ms 32484.
Lynch, Alderman Anthony (d. 1638), Funeral Entry, Ms 70, volume 7, page 547.
Lynch, Christopher (d.1635), Funeral Entry, Ms 69, 1638, page 342.
Lynch, Stephen (d. 1636), Funeral Entry, Ms 70, volume 7, page 30.
Lynch of Galway, Betham Sketch Pedigrees I, IV, Genealogical Office Ms 264, p 45-50.
Pedigree of Lynch afterwards Lynch Blosse of Castlecarra, Clogher, Co Mayo and of Cadiz in Spain, 1250-*c*.1812, Genealogical Office Ms 170, pages 135-139.
Pedigree of Lynch of Athenry, Drimcong, Ballydavid, Lydican and Lynch's Grove, Co Galway and of Paris, *c*.1430-1784. Genealogical Office Ms 165, pages 389-392.
Pedigree of Lynch of Dughisky (Merlin Park), Co Galway and Lynch/Crean Lynch and Lynch of Gahody, *c*.1720-*c*.1800, Genealogical Office Ms 112, page 328 (Burke), page 329 (Browne).
Pedigree of Lynch of Renville, Co Galway, *c*.1600-*c*.1720, Genealogical Office Ms 161, pages 102, 107.

National Archives of Ireland
Crossle genealogical abstracts, card index.
Guinness, Mahon & Co Collection, includes deed of partition of lands in county of the town of Galway & Co Galway & map, Martin Blake Lynch of Dublin & Mark Browne Lynch of Newtown, Co Galway, 16 Aug 1777, Small Accessions Index 59, D 5784-5786 & CO 1075-1076.
J.H. Montgomery & Son, solicitor's collection, includes wills of Mark Lynch of Garracloon 1750 & Martin Blake Lynch of Dublin 1801 & other documents re the partition of lands in 1777. Small Accessions Index 88, T 4020, T 4032, CO 2679-2683, CO 2897-2898, D 12,658.
Prerogative will of Neptune Lynch, 1795, T 19631.
Records and genealogical papers re Lynch family in case of T H Lynch v M Clarkin & others re estate of Charles Lynch (d.1897) of Ballycurrin, Co Mayo and Inchiquin Island, Lough Corrib, 1900, M 6179 (1-141).
Testamentary card index.
Tithe Applotment, Microfilm 38, Kilcummin parish, Co Galway, 11/23, page 14.

General Register Office, Dublin
Index books to marriages, 1845-99.

National University of Ireland, Galway
Galway Corporation statute book (*Liber A*) 1485-1709, Special Collections LA1.

Primary Sources (continued)

Registry of Deeds
Lynch, Philip, re Renville estate to (uncle) John Ormsby of Dublin, book 17, page 337; book 7, page 294; book 18, page 249.

Printed[87]
Blake, M J, 'An Old Lynch Manuscript' *Journal of the Galway Archaeological and Historical Society,* volume 8, 1913-14, pages 65-75.

Blake, M J, 'Account of the Lynch Family Written in 1815' *Journal of the Galway Archaeological and Historical Society,* volume 8, 1913-14, pages 76-93.

Blake, M J, 'An Old Lynch Manuscript' *Journal of the Galway Archaeological and Historical Society,* volume 9, 1915-16, pages 79-107, pedigree after page 107.

Blake, M J, 'Pedigree of Lynch of Lavally, Co Galway' *Journal of the Galway Archaeological and Historical Society,* volume 10, 1917-18, pages 66-69.

Ellis, Eilish and P Beryl Eustace, *Registry of Deeds Dublin: Abstracts of Wills, Vol III, 1785-1832,* Irish Manuscripts Commission, Dublin, 1984, Will 438, Joseph Lynch of Cloonlagheen, Ballyovey (Partry), Co Mayo, 1813, pages 280, 281

Eustace, P Beryl, *Registry of Deeds Dublin: Abstracts of Wills, Vol I, 1708-1745,* Irish Manuscripts Commission, Dublin, 1956, Will of Philip Lynch of Renville, 1716, page 54.

Eustace, P Beryl, *Registry of Deeds Dublin: Abstracts of Wills, Vol II, 1746-85,* Irish Manuscripts Commission, Dublin, 1954, Will 64, Mark Lynch, Garracloon, Co Mayo, 1749, pages 32-3, Will 408, Edmond Bodkin, Kilcloony, Co Galway, 1767, page 201.

Farrar, Henry, *Index to Irish Marriages, 1771-1812,* London, 1897 and Baltimore, 1972 (available in NLI).

Gilbert, J T, *Archives of the Town of Galway* in Hist Mss Comm, 10th Report, Appendix V (The Mss of the Marquis of Ormonde, The Earl of Fingal, The Corporations of Waterford , Galway etc) HMSO, London, 1885, page 380 of 380-520.

Hamilton, H C, *Calendar of state papers, Ireland: 1588-1592, 1592-1596,* London, 1885.

MacLysaght, Edward, 'Report on documents relating to the Wardenship of Galway,' *Analecta Hibernica,* 1944, volume 14, pages 1-249.

Morrin, James, *Calendar of the patent rolls Ireland: Elizabeth V (18th -45th year),* volume 2, Dublin, 1862.

Nicholls, K W, 'The Lynch Blosse Papers,' *Analecta Hibernica,* 1980, volume 29, pages 113-219.

O'Donovan, John, *Annals of the Four Masters,* volume 7, Index, Dublin, 1851.

Ó Muraile, Nollaig, editor, *The great book of Irish genealogies (Leabhar mór na ngenealach)* compiled (1645-66) by Dubhaltach Mac Fhirbhisigh, Dublin, 2003, volume 4, pages 143, 144; volume 5, pages 436, 437.

'Partry private cemetery, Cloonlagheen, Ballyovey,' *Journal of the Association for the Preservation of the Memorials of the Dead in Ireland,* volume 8 (1), pages 131-4.

---

[87]   Listed journals contain unedited transcripts of manuscripts, marriage settlements, pedigrees and/or wills.

Primary Sources (continued)

Simington, Robert C, *The Transplantation to Connacht 1654-58*, Irish Manuscripts Commission, Dublin, 1970, page 124.

Sweetman, H. S, editor, *Calendar of documents, relating to Ireland*, Public Record Office, London, 1171-1307.

The Irish Fiants of the Tudor Sovereigns, volume 3, Queen Elizabeth I, 1586-1603; volume 4, Index-Elizabeth, Dublin 1994.

Irish Architectural Archive

Barna house, Co Galway, photograph, 022/013.

Cloghballymore castle and mansion, Kilcolgan, Co Galway, image in Report for planning, 145/046 & 145/047.

Clogher house, Claremorris, Co Mayo, photograph in sales catalogue of household effects, 24/27, April 1967.

Lynch-Blosse, Athavallie house, Balla, Co Mayo, photograph 2003, 121/010.

Waterdale house, Claregalway, Co Galway, photograph, 022/095.

Internet

John Bodkin, Dominick Bodkin and others-Executed in Ireland on 26th of March, 1742, for the Murder of Eleven Persons, The Newgate Calendar Part II (1742 to 1799), http://www.exclassics.com/newgate/newgate2.txt.

Records 1-30, Letters and Papers, Foreign and Domestic, of the Reign of Henry VIII; records 31, 32, Calendar Mss Salisbury, State Papers Online, Part 1, http://go.galegroup.com/mss/basicSearch.do, Gale, Cengage Learning, 2008, 'Lynch' and 'Lynche.'

Petition on Behalf of Capt Henry Clare, Calendar of the Manuscripts of the Most Hon. the Marquis of Salisbury, Preserved at Hatfield House, Hertfordshire, editor, R. A. Roberts, vol 12, 1602, number 172, London, 1910 State Papers Online, Part 1, http://go.galegroup.com/mss/basicSearch.do.

Photograph 001149, negative 18469, H R Bloss-Lynch, http://www.harrowphotos.com/.

Report of the Mesopotamia Commission, HO 45/10838/331607, http://www.nationalarchives.gov.uk/pathways/firstworldwar/transcripts/battles/meso_comm.htm

Sir Robert Lynch Blosse of Athavallie: grant of burial plot in perpetuity in the parish churchyard of Balla, Co Mayo by Charles Brodrick, Bishop of Tuam, Killalla and Achonry, 11 September 1867 (scan of deed, courtesy of Richard Hely Lynch-Blosse, 17th Bt, 19 May 2009).

Secondary Sources

Reference

Blake, M J, *Blake family records, 1300-1600*, 1st series, London, 1902, Record 69, pages 47-49 of 199.

Blake, M J, 'A transplanter's decree of Final Settlement by the Loughrea Commissioners in Cromwell's time', *Journal of the Galway Archaeological and Historical Society,* 1903-04, volume 3, pages 148-153.

Blake, M J, *Blake family records, 1600-1700*, 2nd ser, London, 1905, pages 240-41 of 297

Blake, M J, 'O'Shaughnessy of Gort (1543-1783): Tabular Pedigree,' *Journal of the Galway Archaeological and Historical Society,* 1909-10, volume 6, pages 58-64.

Blake, M J, 'O'Shaughnessy Tabular Pedigree-Correction,' *Journal of the Galway Archaeological and Historical Society,* 1911-12, volume 7, page 53.

Blake, M J, 'Ballycurren Castle, Co Mayo-families of Lynch of Petersburgh (Ballynonagh) and Lynch of Ballycurren,' *Tuam Herald*, 24 Nov 1917, page 4.

Blake, M J, 'Tabular pedigrees of the D'Arcy family,' *Journal of the Galway Archaeological and Historical Society,* 1917-1918, volume 10, pages 58-66.

Blake, M J, 'Some former Lynch families of Co Galway-pedigrees hitherto unpublished-ancestry of Stanislaus Lynch and his relations,' *Tuam Herald*, 1, 8, 15 December 1928, page 4 in each issue.

Blake, M J, 'Unpublished pedigrees of Lynch families-Lynch of Mount Ross, Headford and Lynch of Ballycurren,' *Tuam Herald*, 22, 29 December 1928, pages 4.

Blake, M J, 'Family of Lynch of Drimcong in Moycullen Barony,' *Tuam Herald*, 12 January 1929, page 4.

Bradshaw, Myrrha and Jacqueline Dowie, *Journal of the Galway Archaeological and Historical Society: Index to Volumes I to VII*, pages 110-2, Dublin, 1913.

Burke, Bernard, *A genealogical and heraldic history of the landed gentry of Ireland*, edited by A C Fox-Davies, London, 1912, 786 pages including 'Athy of Renville,' pages 15, 16; 'Blake of Ballinafad, Co Mayo,' page 51; 'Blake of Tower Hill, Co Mayo,' pages 48-9; 'Ffrench of Monivea,' page 223; 'Lynch of Barna,' page 423; 'Lynch of Duras,' page 423; 'Lynch of Partry,' pages 423-4; 'Martin of Ross,' page 461; 'Moore of Moore Hall,' page 492; 'Lynch-Staunton,' page 658; 'Staunton,' page 653.

Burke, Bernard, *Genealogical and heraldic history of the landed gentry of Ireland*, edited by L.G. Pine, London, 4th edition, 1958, 778 pages, including 'Browne of Moyne Castle,' page 114; 'Darcy of New Forest,' page 164; 'Wilson Lynch of Belvoir formerly of Duras and Renmore,' page 450.

Burke's Peerage and Baronetage, Charles Mosley, editor, Crans, Switzerland, 107th edition, 2003, volume 2, G-O, Lynch-Blosse, pages 2436-38.

Chambers, Anne, *Granuaile (Grace O'Malley): Ireland's Pirate Queen c. 1530-1603*, Dublin, 2003, 205 pages.

Clesham, Brigid, editor, *The register of the parish of St Nicholas, (Church of Ireland) Galway, 1792-1840*, Dublin, 2005, 163 pages.

Figgis, Nicola and Brendan Rooney, *Irish Paintings in the National Gallery of Ireland*, volume 1, Dublin, 2001

Secondary Sources (continued)

Hanks, Patrick and Flavia Hodges, *A Dictionary of Surnames*, Oxford, 1988, 826 pages.

Hardiman, James, *The History of the Town and County of the Town of Galway*, Dublin 1820, 316 pages.

Henry, William, *Role of Honour-The Mayors of Galway City 1485-2001*, Galway City Council, 2002, 312 pages.

Lynam, Shevawn, *Humanity Dick 'King of Connemara' 1754-1834*, Dublin, 1989, 300 p.

McGinn, Brian, 'Che Guevara's Irish blood, The Lynch family of Argentina' *Irish Roots*, 1993, volume 2, pages 11-14.

MacLysaght, Edward, *Irish Families: Their Names, Arms and Origins*, Dublin, 1957, pages 213, 214, Plate XIX.

MacLysaght, Edward, *The Surnames of Ireland*, 5th edition, Dublin, 1980, 309 pages.

Melvin, Patrick, 'The Galway Tribes as Landowners and Gentry', pages 319-74 in *Galway History and Society*, edited by Gerard Moran, Raymond Gillespie and William Nolan, Dublin, 1996, 848 pages.

Moran, Gerard, Raymond Gillespie and William Nolan, editors, *Galway: History & Society*, Dublin, 1996, 848 pages.

Murray, Paul, *From the shadow of Dracula: A life of Bram Stoker*, London, 2004, 340 pages.

Ní Loingsigh, Bernadette, 'Loingsigh Bhordeaux', *Galvia*, 1960, volume 7, pages 4-19.

O'Byrne, Eileen, editor, *The convert rolls*, 1981, Irish Manuscripts Commission, Dublin, 308 pages.

O'Byrne, Eileen and Anne Chamney, editors, *The convert rolls, 1703-1838*, 2005, Irish Manuscripts Commission, Dublin, page 385.

O'Hart, John, *The Irish and Anglo-Irish Landed Gentry*, Irish University Press, Shannon, 1968, page 624 of 774.

Playfair, William, *British Family Antiquity of the Nobility of the United Kingdom containing the Baronetage of Ireland*, London, 1811, including 'Lynch, now Blosse,' pages 51-4.

Vicars, Arthur, *Index to the Prerogative Wills of Ireland 1536-1810*, Dublin, 1897, 512 pages.

General

Blake, M J, 'Ballycurren Castle, Co Mayo-historical notes relating to it,' *Tuam Herald*, 17 November 1917, page 4.

Corish, P J, 'Two contemporary historians of the confederation of Kilkenny: John Lynch and Richard O'Ferrell,' *Irish Historical Studies*, volume 8, pages 217-36.

Cosgrove, Art, editor, *A New history of Ireland. Vol 2, Medieval Ireland 1169-1534*, Oxford, 1987, 982 pages.

'Death of Henry Ffrench Lynch Esq,' *Tuam Herald*, 6 August 1921, page 4.

Lowe, John, editor, *Letter-Book of the Earl of Clanricarde 1643-47*, Irish Manuscripts Commission, Dublin, 1983, 504 pages.

Lynch-Robinson, C H, *The last of the Irish R M's*, London, 1951, 208 pages (available in NLI).

Secondary Sources (continued)

McGinn, Brian, 'How Irish is Montserrat?' *Irish Roots*, 1994, part 1, pages 20-23; part 2, pages 15-17; part 4, pages 20-21.

McHugh, Gerarda 'Lynch's Mill at Bodane,' in *Sylane National School 1852-2002*, pages 111-13 of 272, NUI Galway Library, Special Collections 371.07124174/SYL.

Moody, T W and F X Martin, editors, *The course of Irish history*, Dublin 2001, 462 pages.

O'Connor, Priscilla, 'Irish clerics and Jacobites in early eighteenth-century Paris, 1700-30,' in *The Irish in Europe, 1580-1815*, Thomas O'Connor, editor, Dublin, 2001, pages 75-190 of 219.

Ormsby, C C, 'The Castle and Lynch's House (so called) at Shrule,' *Journal of the Galway Archaeological and Historical Society*, volume 8, 1913-14, pages 224-26, including a note by M J Blake.

O'Neill, T P, 'Surnames of County Galway,' *Irish Roots,* 1994, part 1, pages 26-28.

Seathrún of Dubhros, 'The Killykellys of Cloghballymore,' *Galway Advertiser*, 27 August 1998, page 38

Steed, John, *Brother's Keeper®, version 6.2, Genealogy program for Windows*, Rockford, Michigan, 2005, 78 pages.

Williams, Aoife, *Lynch: This is the History of your Surname*, Ennis, Ireland (in UCD).

Internet

Annals, Lynch, Ballycurrin, http://www.shrule.com, viewed 15 January 2009

Bernard Burke, 'D'arcy of Kiltulla,' in *Burke's Genealogical and Heraldic History of the Landed Gentry*, London, 1847, http://books.google.ie/books.

Burke, Oliver J. *Anecdotes of the Connaught Circuit, from its foundation in 1604 to close upon the present time*, Dublin 1885, pages 86-92 of 357, http://openlibrary.org.

Camilla's genealogy (free access), http://www.links.org/, viewed January 2009.

'Complaints of Ireland,' *New York Times*, 23 November 1879, http://query.nytimes.com/mem/archive-free/pdf.

Family History (free access), http://www.peerage.com/, viewed January 2009.

FamilySearch (free access), http://www.familysearch.org, viewed January 2009.

'From Partry to Persia – the story of the Lynch brothers', *Journal of the South Mayo Family Research Society*, 1991, vol 4, page 23, http://www.mayoancestors.com.

Hugh de Lacy, http://www.britannica.com/EBchecked/topic/371762/Hugh-de-Lacy-1st-lord-of-Meath, viewed 1 March 2009.

Genealogical memoranda relating to the family of Lynch, London, 1883, page 13, will of William Linche of Southampton, 1614 http://www.archive.org/stream/genealogicalmem00unkngoog.

Genealogy, the families database (fee based), http://www.stirnet.com, viewed Jan 2009.

Landed estates, http://www.landedestates.ie/LandedEstates/jsp/family-list.jsp?letter=L, Browne (Cloonfad), Browne (Moyne), Lynch, viewed January 2009.

Lynch database available from paul.mcnulty@ucd.ie at PaulBMcNulty.com on http://www.myfamily.

Secondary Sources (continued)

'Lynch,' in *Oxford Dictionary of National Biography*,
http://www.oxforddnb.com/index.jsp, viewed 6 March 2009.

Lynch, Michel, http://www.sparklingdirect.co.uk/wine/michel-lynch.asp., 10 May 2008.

'Lynch-Blosse,' ProQuest Historical Newspapers, The Irish Times (1859-2007),
http://proquest.umi.com/.

Lynch-Blosse pedigree, familytreemaker.genealogy.com/users/w/o/o/Neil-F-
Woodward/PDFGENEO3.pdf, viewed March 2009.

Martyn, A J, 'The Martin-Eyre Feud, 1652-1748, Part 1,' *Galway Advertiser*, 27 July
2000, page 30, http://www.martinhistory.net/27_July_OldGalway.pdf.

Murphy, Christina, 'Community buys out nuns' school,' *The Irish Times (1874-Current
File)*, 25 August 1976, ProQuest Historical Newspapers, The Irish Times (1859-
2007), page 10, http://proquest.umi.com/.

Murphy, Sean J, A Survey of Irish Surnames 1993-97 (Draft), page 21,
http://homepage.eircom.net/%7Eseanjmurphy/studies/surnames.pdf, 23 Apr 2009.

'Novel Point Raised at Claremorris,' *Weekly Irish Times (1876-1941)*, 3 February, 1912,
ProQuest Historical Newspapers, The Irish Times (1859-2007), page 15,
http://proquest.umi.com/.

O'Connell, Jarlath, The Bodkin murders,
http://places.galwaylibrary.ie/history/chapter77.html, viewed 20 September 2008.

O'Malley, Grace, 1530-1603, http://www.links.org, viewed January 2009.

'The Balla Eviction, Our Special Correspondent,' *The Irish Times (1874-Current File)*;
22 November 1879; ProQuest Historical Newspapers, The Irish Times (1859-
2007), page 5, http://proquest.umi.com/.

Thomas Lynch III, http://www.fdu.com/family/hesignedforus.htm, viewed 28 May 2008.

Todhunter, John, *Life of Patrick Sarsfield*, London, 1895, Patrick Sarsfield, 1st Earl of
Lucan, http://en.wikipedia.org, viewed 1 May 2008.

Viney, Michael, 'Rights In Common,' *The Irish Times (1874-Current File)*, 3 March
1979, ProQuest Historical Newspapers, The Irish Times (1859-2007), page 10,
http://proquest.umi.com/,

Welsh Farmers at the Agricultural College Glasnevin, *Weekly Irish Times (1876-1941)*,
24 September 1910, ProQuest Historical Newspapers, The Irish Times (1859-
2007), page 12, http://proquest.umi.com/.

Will of Sir Robert Lynchblosse, *The Irish Times (1874-Current File)*, 26 February 1894,
ProQuest Historical Newspapers, The Irish Times (1859-2007), page 5,
http://proquest.umi.com/.

William III of England, http://en.wikipedia.org, viewed 3 December 2008.

Index

Index (contd)

Index (contd)

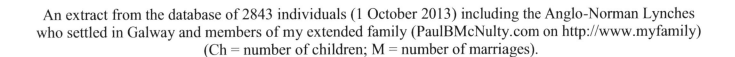

An extract from the database of 2843 individuals (1 October 2013) including the Anglo-Norman Lynches who settled in Galway and members of my extended family (PaulBMcNulty.com on MyFamily.com)

An extract from the database of 2843 individuals (1 October 2013) including the Anglo-Norman Lynches who settled in Galway and members of my extended family (PaulBMcNulty.com on http://www.myfamily) (Ch = number of children; M = number of marriages).

Num	Name	Birth date	Died	Father	Spouse	Married	Ch	M
521	Acton, Phyllis				Martin '. Fallon		5	1
3062	Adams, Lucy Myra		1988		G R. Lynch-Blosse		1	1
416	Aherne, Alexandra			158				
158	Aherne, Michael '.				Valeria Cleere	5 May 2005	1	1
1817	Alexander, King II S.						1	1
457	Alldritt, Frederick				Anne Fallon			1
2152	Arthur, Nicholas (Sir)				Margaret Blake			1
2034	Athy, Andrew			2023				
2013	Athy, Andrew (Capt)			2019	Anastacia Joyce		1	1
2035	Athy, Catherine '.			2023				
2048	Athy, Catherine '.			2040				
709	Athy, Catherine More			711	Peter 'Piers Penrise		1	1
2029	Athy, Christopher			2003				
2003	Athy, Edmond			2013	Margaret Lynch		7	1
2019	Athy, Edmond				Margaret Lynch		1	1
2030	Athy, Edmond			2003				
2052	Athy, Edmond J P	2 Jun 1859		2046	Annette F. Gradwell	25 Oct 1881	1	1
2033	Athy, Edmond Lynch			2023	??? Nottingham		2	1
2041	Athy, Eleanor			2033	E Taaffe			1
2412	Athy, Elizabeth Mary	c. 1818	20 Apr 1863/45	2040				
2002	Athy, Jane	c.1700		2003	John Moore	c.1727	3	1
2036	Athy, Jane			2023				
2024	Athy, John			2003				
711	Athy, John More						1	1
1265	Athy, Margaret				Stephen Lynch		2	1
692	Athy, Mary 'Maria'				Thomas Lynch		1	1
2053	Athy, Mary Elizabeth			2046	Frederick Hounsell	28 Apr 1889	1	1
2059	Athy, Muriel Pauline			2052				
2047	Athy, Myles (Rev)		Oct 1892	2040				
2025	Athy, Oliver			2003	??? Skerrett			1
2040	Athy, Philip Edmond		18 May 1840	2033	Bridget MacDonnell		4	1
2023	Athy, Philip Lynch		c.1774	2003	Eleanor French		4	1
2046	Athy, Randal Edmd L.	1814	10 Apr 1875	2040	Margaret Buckle	27 Apr 1858	2	1
2031	Athy, Sarah			2003				
3006	Atkinson, ???				Ellinor Moore			1
539	Audley, Edmond 'Adley'	c 1815					1	1
71	Audley, Mary 'Adley'	c.1847		539	Michael Toole	24 Feb 1867	1	1
3085	Baddeley, Nadine				David Lynch-Blosse	1989	1	1
2429	Balcombe, Florence	1858	1937		Abraham '. Stoker	1878		1
973	Banks, Charles Edward						1	1
972	Banks, Frances Dorothy			973	Robert Lynch-Blosse	16 Apr 1932		1
822	Barker, Elizabeth Jane	1728	1756/28y	823	Robert (6th Lynch	14 Jan 1749	2	1
823	Barker, Francis	c.1698	23 Mar 1734/36		Cecilia Blosse		2	1
3100	Barker, Thomas	c.1721-22	9 Sep 1736/14y	823				
2182	Barnewall, Bridget	c.1723	2 Feb 1762	2183	Robert Martin	6 Apr 1753	2	1
2183	Barnewall, John (11th	1672	7 Apr 1746		Mary ? M. Barnewall	1703	1	1
2184	Barnewall, Mary ? M.	c.1682	1 Nov 1771		John (11th Barnewall	1703	1	1
2805	Barradaele, Joseph				Agnes Lynch	8 Nov 1817		1
1469	Barry, Margaret				Dermot O'Shaughnessy	1733	2	1
3058	Barry, Peter						1	1
3057	Barry, Peter James			3058	Bridget Lynch-Blosse	9 Dec 2000	2	1
1733	Barry, Viscount David				Gyles or Julia ZZ?		1	1
3079	Bate, Leonard Arthur R		22 Mar 1959		C. Lynch-Blosse	7 Dec 1918		1
2011	Baynham, George						1	1
2010	Baynham, Margaret			2011	Philip Lynch		2	1
2214	Bell, Arthur Gonne				Mary L '. Martin	14 Sep 1847		1
1001	Bellew, Christopher			999	Barbara Dillon		3	1
1003	Bellew, Christopher			1001	Olivia ZZ?		1	1
1005	Bellew, Henry			1001				
1010	Bellew, Jane			1007				
999	Bellew, John						1	1
1006	Bellew, Luke		1819	1001				
1007	Bellew, Michael (1st			1003	Helena ZZ?		2	1

An extract from the database of 2843 individuals (1 October 2013) including the Anglo-Norman Lynches who settled in Galway and members of my extended family (PaulBMcNulty.com on http://www.myfamily) (Ch = number of children; M = number of marriages).

Num	Name	Birth date	Died	Father	Spouse	Married	Ch	M
1009	Bellew, William		c 1855	1007				
209	Bergin, Margaret				Peter McHugh		4	1
2385	Bermingham, ???						2	1
269	Bermingham, ???	c 1835			Michael Griffin		3	1
1424	Bermingham, Christiane				John Lynch		1	1
1760	Bermingham, Edmond				Joan O'Shaughnessy	c.1560	1	1
2386	Bermingham, Edward			2385				
2362	Bermingham, Francis						1	1
2310	Bermingham, Jane		6 Jun 1687	2362	Myles 'Miles' Burke		1	1
2384	Bermingham, John			2385	Elizabeth Darcy			1
1761	Bermingham, Richard	1570	1645	1760				
2659	Bernard, Francis				Frieda Ottman	1922		1
1806	Bethune, Alice 'de'				William Marshal	Sep 1214		1
2947	Beytagh, Edward (QC)				Margaret Lynch		2	1
2949	Beytagh, Elizabeth			2947				
2948	Beytagh, Margaret			2947				
1948	Biggs, Jane			1949	Marcus 'Mark' Lynch		2	1
1949	Biggs, Nicholas						1	1
1827	Bigod, Hugh (Earl N.				Maude M. Marshal	1206	1	1
1828	Bigod, Roger (Earl M.			1827				
2466	Bingham, ???			2467	George (2nd Browne		1	1
2467	Bingham, Henry (Bt)						1	1
976	Bircham, Cicely Edith			977	Henry Lynch-Blosse	17 Feb 1914		1
977	Bircham, Francis T.						1	1
2237	Blackeney, Anne				Evan S. Martin	9 Nov 1859		1
2247	Blackeney, Catherine	abt 1842			Frederick O. Martin	1 Jan 1862		1
1287	Blake, ???				James (Mayor) Lynch		2	1
1512	Blake, ???				Edmond or E. Blake		1	1
1853	Blake, ???				Patrick French			1
624	Blake, ???						1	1
1612	Blake, Agnes 'Ines'			1701	Patrick Lynch		7	1
1862	Blake, Anastacia '.		1771	2521	Michael Lynch	1740	1	1
919	Blake, Andrew						2	1
2154	Blake, Anne			2145	Richard Darcy			1
1856	Blake, Anstace			1857	Joseph Lynch	1712	1	1
615	Blake, Anstace		Mar 1766	941	Marcus Lynch	1742	3	1
2502	Blake, Anstace '.			2503	William Browne		1	1
2983	Blake, Bridget			2984	Dominick Darcy			1
1610	Blake, Catherine				William Lynch		1	1
1655	Blake, Catherine			1656	Martin Darcy	20 May 1653	2	1
2064	Blake, Catherine			2065	Henry Crean	1703	1	1
2828	Blake, Catherine				Thomas ? Lynch		1	1
2977	Blake, Catherine			2978	Richard Darcy		1	1
565	Blake, Catherine			566	Stephen Lynch		7	1
621	Blake, Catherine			622	Nicholas Lynch	1765	3	1
766	Blake, Catherine		21 Oct 1749	767	Robert (4th Lynch	29 Nov 1683	7	1
951	Blake, Catherine			650	Arthur 'O O'Connor	Mar 1853		1
2759	Blake, Celia			2760	Isidore Lynch			1
1511	Blake, Edmond or E.			919	??? Blake		1	1
3038	Blake, Edward							
1767	Blake, Eveline			1768	Peter 'Pyerse' Lynch	1468		1
914	Blake, F						1	1
2579	Blake, Frances			2580	Arthur Henry Lynch	18 Nov 1812	5	1
918	Blake, Frances		1843	919	John Darcy	4 Jun 1804		1
1969	Blake, Francis	7 Feb 1789			Georgina E. Burke	19 Jan 1819	1	1
2148	Blake, Francis			2145				
2420	Blake, George	Jul 1700	11 Sep 1771	2421	Julia '. Lynch	18 Apr 1728	3	1
2423	Blake, George		8 Sep 1798	2422				
1396	Blake, Harriet			1397	Francis Lynch		4	1
1770	Blake, Henry						1	1
622	Blake, Henry			624			1	1
767	Blake, Henry		c.1703				2	1
865	Blake, Henry				Catherine Gibson		1	1

Num	Name	Birth date	Died	Father	Spouse	Married	Ch	M
2580	Blake, Isidore						2	1
796	Blake, Isidore			1561	Jane Lynch			1
931	Blake, Isidore or M.						1	1
1561	Blake, John						1	1
1768	Blake, John			1770			1	1
1865	Blake, John			1857			1	1
1968	Blake, John	c.1826	c.1880	1969	Mary Lynch-Staunton	1861		1
2257	Blake, John				Ann Hamilton			1
2774	Blake, John				Mary Lynch			1
1405	Blake, John H				Harriet Lynch			1
2765	Blake, Joseph S				Frances Lynch			1
1867	Blake, Julia			937	Francis Lynch		7	1
1066	Blake, Julia 'Julian'			741				
2149	Blake, Julia 'Juliane'			2145	Adam Font			1
2430	Blake, Marcus 'Mark'		bef 1799	2420	Mary O'Donnell		1	1
2998	Blake, Marcus 'Mark'			2430				
933	Blake, Marcus 'Mark'		c.1810	937	Christian Kirwan	c.1777	1	1
941	Blake, Marcus 'Mark'			1857	Julia Kirwan	c.1712	2	1
1457	Blake, Margaret			1458	Thomas ? Lynch		7	1
2151	Blake, Margaret			2145	Nicholas Arthur			2
2511	Blake, Margaret				Joseph Lynch		8	1
2571	Blake, Margaret			2572	Joseph Lynch	1675	4	1
2877	Blake, Margaret			2878	Christopher French	1 Nov 1686		2
797	Blake, Margaret				Henry Lynch			1
1067	Blake, Margaret '.			742	James Lynch		2	1
3153	Blake, Margaret '.				Oliver Bodkin	c. 1732	1	1
1864	Blake, Margaret Maria		c.1783	1865	Joseph Lynch	1766	2	1
2233	Blake, Martin				Margaret Martin			1
2421	Blake, Martin						1	1
2572	Blake, Martin fitz A.						1	1
2791	Blake, Martin J (MRIA)	1853	1931					
1988	Blake, Mary			650	George Henry Moore	1851	4	1
648	Blake, Mary			931	Marcus Lynch	24 Jan 1794	1	1
748	Blake, Mary		c.1712	749	Henry (3rd Bt) Lynch		5	1
776	Blake, Mary			1511	Patrick Lynch	8 May 1780	5	1
913	Blake, Mary			914	Hyacinth Darcy			1
2433	Blake, Matilda			2422	Thomas Thornley	3 Oct 1817	2	1
1857	Blake, Maurice				Anastacia '. Darcy		3	1
650	Blake, Maurice		1852	933	Anne Lynch	1815	2	1
937	Blake, Maurice		c.1779	941	Sibilla French	c.1733	2	1
749	Blake, Nicholas						1	1
1701	Blake, Patrick				Catherine Browne		1	1
2521	Blake, Patrick						1	1
2254	Blake, Peter				Mary French			1
2760	Blake, Peter			2580			1	1
2878	Blake, Peter						1	1
3046	Blake, Peter			767				
2978	Blake, Peter (Major)						1	1
1351	Blake, Pierce				Eleanor Lynch	20 Feb 1737		1
1397	Blake, Pierce ?						1	1
2422	Blake, Richard	31 May 1736	1801	2420	Elizabeth O'Donnell		2	1
1656	Blake, Richard (Bt)						1	1
658	Blake, Richard (Sir)			566				
566	Blake, Robert						2	1
2984	Blake, Stephen						1	1
2881	Blake, Surna				Hyacinth French	22 Mar 1703	1	1
2826	Blake, Sybil				Isidore (Col) Lynch		2	1
2065	Blake, Thomas						1	1
2160	Blake, Thomas	20 Jan 1574		2162			1	1
756	Blake, Thomas			865	Mary Lynch			1
742	Blake, Thomas (2nd Bt)			2145	Julia '. Browne		2	1
1062	Blake, Thomas (4th Bt)		1676	741	Mary Martin	1649		3
2162	Blake, Valentine		1499		Evelyn '. Lynch		1	1

An extract from the database of 2843 individuals (1 October 2013) including the Anglo-Norman Lynches who settled in Galway and members of my extended family (PaulBMcNulty.com on http://www.myfamily) (Ch = number of children; M = number of marriages).

Num	Name	Birth date	Died	Father	Spouse	Married	Ch	M
2503	Blake, Valentine				Eveline French		1	1
2145	Blake, Valentine (1st	1560	2 Jan 1634	2158	Margaret French		5	2
741	Blake, Valentine (3rd	1608	1652	742	Eleanor '. Lynch	27 Jun 1632	2	1
1458	Blake, Walter						1	1
2158	Blake, Walter			2160	Julia '. Browne	1573	1	1
763	Blake, Walter							2
2473	Blake, Walter fitz A.				Anastacia Bodkin			1
2569	Blosse, Cecilia	c. 1698	2 Jul 1740/42y	2570	Francis Barker		2	1
3059	Blosse, Charles James	1994		3057				
3060	Blosse, Django Peter	2000		3057				
2570	Blosse, Thomas		23 May 1722		Cecilia Tyrell		2	1
3101	Blosse, Tobias	23 Mar 1697	1 Nov 1737/40y	2570				
1278	Bodkin, ???				1279 Stephen Lynch	1518	3	1
2460	Bodkin, ???				2457 ??? Lynch		1	1
2607	Bodkin, ???				Henry Lynch	1579	1	1
2824	Bodkin, ???						2	1
2838	Bodkin, ???				Julia Lynch			1
1022	Bodkin, Aileen Cox	1886/7	1979	1023	Thomas Bodkin		1	1
2472	Bodkin, Anastacia				2867 James 'Rivagh' Darcy		3	2
1650	Bodkin, Anna				Marcus 'Joyes' Joyce		1	1
1014	Bodkin, Arabella N.		1931	1017	Mathias M Bodkin		6	1
2464	Bodkin, Dominick '.		8 Oct 1741	2450				
3155	Bodkin, Dominick '.		3 May 1739	2452				
2825	Bodkin, Edmond			2824				
2821	Bodkin, Elinor			2824	??? Lynch		1	1
1031	Bodkin, Emma		1950	1013	??? Norman			1
3156	Bodkin, Francis '.		c.1740	2452				
2457	Bodkin, Hyacinth			2456	Isabella '. Lynch		1	1
1279	Bodkin, John				Janet Mares		1	1
2450	Bodkin, John		1699		Mary Skerrett		3	2
2452	Bodkin, John '.			2450	Mary Clarke		4	1
2455	Bodkin, John 'Oge'		20 Mar 1742	2452				
2447	Bodkin, John 'Shawn'	c. 1720	8 Oct 1741	2446				
2867	Bodkin, Marcus						1	1
1035	Bodkin, Margaret			1013	J J Robinson			1
1034	Bodkin, Mary R (Sr T.		1955	1013				
1013	Bodkin, Mathias M	1849	1933	1011	Arabella N. Bodkin		6	1
1033	Bodkin, Matthew (Rev)			1013				
1030	Bodkin, Norah (Sr J.		1929	1013				
2446	Bodkin, Oliver		19 Sep 1741	2450	Mary 'Marie' Lynch	c. 1720	2	2
2449	Bodkin, Oliver	1733	19 Sep 1741	2446				
2454	Bodkin, Patrick			2452			1	1
1015	Bodkin, Patrick (Dr)			1011				
1257	Bodkin, Richard				Joan 'Joanna' Lynch			1
1021	Bodkin, Thomas	1887	1961	1013	Aileen Cox Bodkin		1	1
2456	Bodkin, Thomas			2454			1	1
1011	Bodkin, Thomas (Dr)				Maria McDonnell	16 May 1843	2	1
1824	Bohun, Humphrey 'de'						1	1
1823	Bohun, Maud 'de'			1824	Anselm Marshal			1
407	Bolger, ???			409	Mary ? Murphy		1	1
409	Bolger, ???						1	1
403	Bolger, Joseph			407	Julia Hendrick	c 1927	1	1
155	Bolger, Juliett	19 Jan 1931		403	Thomas F McHugh	24 Sep 1956	5	1
2908	Bonfield, Michael				Monica Lynch	7 Feb 1752		1
1403	Boothman, C? T				Mary Lynch			1
389	Boylan, ???						1	1
53	Boylan, Agnes C.		19 Dec 1874	24				
52	Boylan, Eustace (Rev)	c 1867	c 1950	24				
30	Boylan, James?	c 1790		389	Margaret ZZ?		1	1
24	Boylan, John	c 1822	7 Nov 1874	30	Margaret Kavanagh	c.1861	6	1
44	Boylan, John Jr	c 1865	6 May 1925/60y	24				
5	Boylan, Mary	c.1863	22 Nov 1945/82	24	Thomas McNulty	30 Dec 1891	4	1
43	Boylan, Stephen James	c 1871	13 Jan 1908	24				

An extract from the database of 2843 individuals (1 October 2013) including the Anglo-Norman Lynches who settled in Galway and members of my extended family (PaulBMcNulty.com on http://www.myfamily) (Ch = number of children; M = number of marriages).

Num	Name	Birth date	Died	Father	Spouse	Married	Ch	M
45	Boylan, Teresa Mary	8 Dec 1865	10 Feb 1949/83	24				
364	Boyle, Anne				Martin Fallon		9	1
439	Boyle, Bridget							
1107	Boyle, James							
348	Boyle, Maria							
438	Boyle, Patrick							
1104	Boyle, Patrick ?							
2468	Brabazon, Bridget			2469	Nicholas Lynch	1719		1
2469	Brabazon, William				Mary Browne		1	1
1838	Braose, William 'de'		1230		Eve/Eva Marshal	bef 1219		1
2639	Briscoe, Edward						1	1
2638	Briscoe, Helen			2639	Stanislaus J. Lynch		5	1
352	Broderick?, ???				??? Flynn	c 1830	1	1
3151	Brooke, Mary	1608	1683		Thomas 'More' Moore		1	1
1129	Broome, Cecilia				Colm Sullivan	10 Nov 2007		1
2074	Browne, ???			1521	Thomas Lynch	1782	4	1
2088	Browne, ???			2089	Marcus 'Mark' Lynch		4	1
2918	Browne, ???						3	1
792	Browne, ??? 'Brown'						2	1
794	Browne, ??? 'Brown'			792				
2718	Browne, Alicia			2719	Henry Lynch	8 Dec 1840		1
1731	Browne, Andrew fitz							
3071	Browne, Anne		21 Feb 1815	828	Ross Mahon	12 Oct 1762		1
2081	Browne, Arthur						1	1
790	Browne, Arthur 'Brown'			792			1	1
1702	Browne, Catherine				Patrick Blake		1	1
2069	Browne, Catherine			1521				
609	Browne, Catherine '.				Nicholas Lynch		3	1
2920	Browne, Cecilia		1762-77	2918	Thomas Lynch			1
2122	Browne, Christian				Thomas (1st Burke		1	1
1060	Browne, Dominick			739				
857	Browne, Dominick				Harriet '. Lynch	18 Nov 1754	1	1
2496	Browne, Dominick		1596	2501	??? O'Flaherty		2	1
1558	Browne, Dominick (Sir)		1656	1064	Anastacia Darcy		2	1
3055	Browne, Dominick G.	1755	8 May 1826	857				
1555	Browne, Eleanor			1556	Stephen fitz Lynch	c 1655	1	1
1301	Browne, Elizabeth			1722	Geoffrey (MP) Lynch		5	1
605	Browne, Elizabeth			606	Marcus Lynch	1684	1	1
1064	Browne, Geoffrey				Mary McMorrishe		3	2
739	Browne, Geoffrey '.		14 Jan 1668		Mary Lynch		2	1
820	Browne, Geoffrey '.				Elizabeth '. Lynch			1
2471	Browne, Geoffrey			1558				
2721	Browne, George				Margaret ZZ?		1	1
2465	Browne, George (2nd		1698	1556	??? Bingham		1	1
875	Browne, Harriet	1827	29 Jun 1904	876	Robert Lynch-Blosse	31 Mar 1853	6	1
827	Browne, Henry		Mar 1812	828	Anne Lynch			1
876	Browne, Howe P (2nd				Hester Cath Burke	4 Mar 1816	1	1
2499	Browne, Jane			2496	Patrick Kirwan			1
2265	Browne, Jennet			2266	Anthony Darcy		1	1
1541	Browne, Joan				Stephen fitz Lynch		3	1
1854	Browne, Joan			1556	Arthur Lynch		1	1
1992	Browne, John						1	1
1556	Browne, John (1st Bt)		1670		Mary Browne	1626	4	1
2365	Browne, John (Colonel)	1638	1711		Maud 'Bourke' Burke	1669	1	1
828	Browne, John (Ld A.	c.1709	4 July 1776		Anne Gore	Dec 1729	2	1
1520	Browne, Julia		aft 1819	1521	Dominick Crean-Lynch	1784	6	1
743	Browne, Julia 'Julian'			1064	Thomas (2nd Blake		2	1
2159	Browne, Julia '.				Walter Blake	1573	1	1
2080	Browne, Julia ?			2081	Maurice Lynch		4	1
1991	Browne, Louisa			1992	George Moore	Sep 1807	1	1
2332	Browne, Mabel			1556	Brian '. O'Flaherty	1681	3	1
2720	Browne, Margaret			2721	Henry Lynch		4	1
2916	Browne, Margaret		bef Nov 1762	2918	??? Lynch			1

Num	Name	Birth date	Died	Father	Spouse	Married	Ch	M
2962	Browne, Margaret '.				James Darcy			1
2170	Browne, Margery			2171	Nicholas Martin			1
1521	Browne, Martin						3	1
1539	Browne, Martin				Jane Crean-Lynch			1
1720	Browne, Martin			1722	Mary 'Maria' Lynch		1	1
2719	Browne, Martin						1	1
1557	Browne, Mary			1558	John (1st Bt) Browne	1626	4	1
1608	Browne, Mary				Michael Lynch		1	1
2252	Browne, Mary		27 Feb 1631	1064	Peter (Sir) French		4	1
2308	Browne, Mary		bef 1731	2365	Theobold (6th Burke	8 Jul 1702	3	1
2470	Browne, Mary			2465	William Brabazon		1	1
2869	Browne, Mary			2870	Richard Darcy		1	1
770	Browne, Mary 'Brown'			771	John Lynch		7	1
789	Browne, Mary 'Brown'			790	Robert Lynch			1
2870	Browne, Nicholas						1	1
2919	Browne, Nicholas		1762-77	2918				
606	Browne, Oliver (Capt)		c.1686?	1720	Julia Lynch	c.1655	1	1
1722	Browne, Oliver (Mayor)			2496			2	1
1061	Browne, Paul			739				
2171	Browne, Robert						1	1
2266	Browne, Robert						1	1
2506	Browne, Stephen				Evelyn '. Lynch		1	1
2089	Browne, Thomas						1	1
2425	Browne, Thomas				Mary Lynch			1
860	Browne, Valentine							1
771	Browne, Valentine '.						1	1
2501	Browne, William				2506 Anstace '. Blake		1	1
3104	Brownrigg, Eva Lilian							
2049	Buckle, Margaret		31 Mar 1891	2050	Randal Edmd L. Athy	27 Apr 1858	2	1
2050	Buckle, William Hill						1	1
3094	Burke, ?				? Courtney		1	1
3095	Burke, ?			3094	? Treacy		1	1
265	Burke, ???	c 1800					2	1
550	Burke, ???						2	1
415	Burke, ??? 'Bourke'				Mary ZZ?			1
549	Burke, Anne	c 1860		550	John Donoghue		1	1
1546	Burke, Barbara		bef 1792	1544	Marcus 'Mark' Lynch	Mar 1785	1	1
1235	Burke, Catherine							
1376	Burke, Catherine			1371	??? Hynes			2
2369	Burke, Catherine '.			2370	Owen O'Flaherty		1	1
2341	Burke, Catherine or			2342	Timothy O'Flaherty		2	1
1370	Burke, Celia			1371	Anthony Lynch	27 Jul 1801	6	1
1670	Burke, Christopher				Margaret Burke		1	1
1364	Burke, Clara			1354				
2322	Burke, David				Flania O'Flaherty		1	1
1549	Burke, Dominick			1552	Barbara Lynch			1
2370	Burke, Edmond						1	1
1354	Burke, Edward						6	1
2477	Burke, Eleanor			2478	James Lynch			1
2120	Burke, Elizabeth			2121	John (13th E) Burke	17 Mar 1799	1	1
2338	Burke, F? 'Bourke'			2339	Brian '. O'Flaherty		1	1
1204	Burke, Francis							
1970	Burke, Georgina E.			1971	Francis Blake	19 Jan 1819	1	1
877	Burke, Hester Cath 'de	c.1800	17 Feb 1878	2119	Howe P (2nd Browne	4 Mar 1816	1	1
2395	Burke, Honora			2410	Ulick (3rd E. Burke	25 Nov 1564	1	1
2136	Burke, Honora 'Bourke'	16 Jan 1674	16 Jan 1697	2129	Patrick Sarsfield	c.1691	1	2
2314	Burke, Honora 'Bourke'			2315	Myles 'Miles' Burke		1	1
2336	Burke, Honora 'Bourke'				Murrough O'Flaherty		1	1
2371	Burke, Honora 'Bourke'			2372	Murrough O'Flaherty		8	1
2400	Burke, Honora 'Bourke'			2401	Ulick (1st E. Burke			1
1373	Burke, Honora 'Honor'			1371	Thomas Tighe			1
1832	Burke, Hubert 'de B.						1	1
2306	Burke, Joan or Jane		aft 1728	2307	Murrough O'Flaherty	28 Aug 1727	1	1

An extract from the database of 2843 individuals (1 October 2013) including the Anglo-Norman Lynches who settled in Galway and members of my extended family (PaulBMcNulty.com on http://www.myfamily) (Ch = number of children; M = number of marriages).

Num	Name	Birth date	Died	Father	Spouse	Married	Ch	M
2410	Burke, John						1	1
2406	Burke, John 'Bourke'			2397				
2119	Burke, John (13th E)	22 Sep 1744	27 Jul 1808/63	2123	Elizabeth Burke	17 Mar 1799	1	1
2368	Burke, John (8th Vt)		12 Jan 1767	2307				
2127	Burke, John (9th Earl)	1642	17 Oct 1722	2129	Mary Talbot	Oct 1684	1	1
2315	Burke, John (Sir) '.	bef 1589					1	1
2339	Burke, John (Sir) '.						1	1
2123	Burke, John Smith	11 Nov 1720	21 Apr 1782/61	2125	Hester A. Vincent	1 Jul 1740	1	1
1122	Burke, Joseph							
2806	Burke, Judith				Richard Lynch	8 Jul 1820		1
1358	Burke, Julia			1354	Patrick Fitzgerald		3	1
553	Burke, Lena	c 1885		552	John Dooley	c 1905	1	1
1353	Burke, Margaret			1354	Martin Lynch		8	1
1671	Burke, Margaret				Christopher Burke		1	1
2366	Burke, Margaret '.		dsp	2311	Henry (3rd Bt) Lynch			1
2374	Burke, Margaret '.			2375	Murrough O'Flaherty			1
1831	Burke, Margaret 'de			1832	Richard 'de' Clare			1
3009	Burke, Margaret or M.			3010	Garrett (Col) Moore			1
1123	Burke, Mary							
1363	Burke, Mary			1354				
1461	Burke, Mary			1462	William Lynch		1	1
2215	Burke, Mary	c 1773			Patrick Kirwan		1	1
2924	Burke, Mary 'Maria'		c.1624	2342	??? 'More' Moore		2	1
2364	Burke, Maud 'Bourke'	1642		2311	John Browne	1669	1	1
1368	Burke, Michael				Joan 'Joanna' Lynch	1766		1
2125	Burke, Michael (10th	c.1686	29 Nov 1726	2127	Anne Smith	19 Sep 1714	1	1
1543	Burke, Myles			1552	Mary Lynch	1718	1	1
2313	Burke, Myles 'Miles'	bef 1615	1649	2316	Honora '. Burke		1	1
2309	Burke, Myles 'Miles'		Mar 1681	2311	Jane Bermingham		1	1
552	Burke, Patrick 'Pat'	c 1858		550			1	1
1971	Burke, Richard				Johanna Wallscourt		1	1
2372	Burke, Richard '.						1	1
2342	Burke, Richard (2nd		24 Jul 1582	2397	Margaret O'Brien	24 Nov 1553	3	1
3010	Burke, Richard (6th		Aug 1666		Elizabeth Butler		1	1
2353	Burke, Richard Devil's				Margaret O'Flaherty			1
2319	Burke, Richard in Iron		1583	2322	Grace O'Malley	1566	1	1
2404	Burke, Richard M.				Margaret Butler	Apr 1530	1	1
1669	Burke, Sarah			1670	Thomas Redington	1763	1	1
1544	Burke, Stephen			1543	Margery Martin	c.1760	1	1
815	Burke, Theobold				Catherine Lynch			1
2478	Burke, Theobold '.						1	1
2316	Burke, Theobold (1st	1567	18 Jun 1629	2319	Maud O'Connor		1	1
2311	Burke, Theobold (3rd		15 Jan 1653	2313	Elinor ? E. Talbot	aft Sep 163	4	1
2363	Burke, Theobold (4th		1676 dsp	2311				
2307	Burke, Theobold (6th	6 Jan 1681	25 Jun 1741	2309	Mary Browne	8 Jul 1702	3	1
2367	Burke, Theobold (7th	c.1707	7 Jan 1741/42	2307				
1371	Burke, Thomas						3	1
2121	Burke, Thomas (1st Bt)				Christian Browne		1	1
1462	Burke, Thomas						1	1
1552	Burke, Ulick		17 Jan 1711		Catherine '. Lynch		2	1
2397	Burke, Ulick (1st E.		19 Oct 1544	2404	Grace '. O'Carroll		2	3
2394	Burke, Ulick (3rd E.		20 May 1601	2342	Honora Burke	25 Nov 1564	1	1
1365	Burke, Walter				Mary French			1
2375	Burke, Walter 'Bourke'			1354			1	1
426	Burke, William '.							
2129	Burke, William (7th		Oct 1687	2134	Lettice Shirley		2	2
2134	Burke, William (Sir)		2 Feb 1625	2394	Joan O'Shaughnessy		1	1
1356	Burke, Winifred			1354	??? Nolan			1
2109	Bushell, John				Mary Lynch			1
2680	Butler, Charles (RC)						1	1
2133	Butler, Eleanor				Donough (1st McCarty		1	1
2980	Butler, Elizabeth			2981	Dominick Darcy		1	1
3011	Butler, Elizabeth				Richard (6th Burke		1	1

An extract from the database of 2843 individuals (1 October 2013) including the Anglo-Norman Lynches who settled in Galway and members of my extended family (PaulBMcNulty.com on http://www.myfamily) (Ch = number of children; M = number of marriages).

Num	Name	Birth date	Died	Father	Spouse	Married	Ch	M
2981	Butler, James						1	1
2405	Butler, Margaret		Apr 1530	2407	Richard M. Burke	Apr 1530	1	1
2407	Butler, Peter 'Piers'				Margaret Fitzgerald		1	1
2153	Butler, Theobald				Margaret Blake			1
2679	Butler, Theresa		1872	2680	Andrew Henry Lynch			1
597	Byellagh, ???			596				
656	Byellagh, ???			596				
596	Byellagh?, Edward				Mary Lynch		2	1
136	Byrne, Brigid				Patrick McHugh			1
627	Byrne, Jane-Mary			628	Marcus Blake Lynch	Jan 1792		1
628	Byrne, Mark						1	1
2535	Byrne, Nora				Benin Lynch		1	1
1154	Callanan, John '.				Catherine Kearney			1
305	Callanan, Patrick '.							
287	Carroll, Nora				Christopher O'Brien		1	1
480	Caulfield?, ???				James ? Fallon		5	1
870	Causland, Catherine			871	William C. Plunkett		1	1
871	Causland, John						1	1
302	Census, Thomas Farrell							
2141	Churchill, Arabella	23 Feb 1647	4 May 1730/83y	2533	James II Stuart	1665	1	1
2533	Churchill, Winston				Elizabeth Drake		1	1
283	Clancy, Catherine				Joseph O'Brien		2	1
1829	Clare, Gilbert (Earl)		1230		Isabel Marshal	9 Oct 1217	1	1
1796	Clare, Isabel 'de'	c 1172	1220	1797	William Marshal	1189	10	1
1830	Clare, Richard 'de'		1262	1829	Margaret 'de Burke			2
1797	Clare, Richard S.	1130	20 Apr 1176		Aoife MacMurrough	1170	1	1
2453	Clarke, Mary				John '. Bodkin		4	1
1603	Clavering, ???			1602				
1602	Clavering, Ralph				Guillemette Lynch		1	1
162	Cleary, Geraldine				Thomas McHugh	22 Sep 1992	3	1
159	Cleere, Maria			180				
157	Cleere, Valeria			180	Michael '. Aherne	5 May 2005	1	1
180	Cleere, William				Anne Marie McHugh	c.1978	2	1
332	Coen, Bridget							
331	Coen, Darby							
334	Coen, Dermot							
340	Coen, Eleanor							
272	Coen, Mary 'Maria'	c 1825			John 'Lahey' Leahy	c 1847	8	1
342	Coen, Mary 'Maria'							
339	Coen, Michael							
2771	Cole, ??? (Major)						1	1
2770	Cole, William de Vere			2771	Denise Daly	30 Sep 1918		1
2761	Coleman, ???				Isidore Lynch		1	1
488	Collins, ???				Charles Fallon			1
1985	Collins, Benjamin						1	1
1984	Collins, Jane			1985	George L Staunton		1	1
1149	Collins, Margaret		6 May 1946		Thomas Kearney			1
3148	Colt, Johanna 'Joan,	1488	1511		Thomas 'More' Moore		1	1
1119	Commins, Mary							
2114	Comyn, David		20 Dec 1776		Dorothea McNamara	8 Feb 1762	1	1
954	Comyn, Laurence		28 Jun 1819	2114	Jane Lynch	24 Mar 1800		1
3092	Connaughton, Lenny				Lucy ŻZ?			1
76	Conneely, Barbara '.			61				
3141	Conneely, Barbara '.			63				
78	Conneely, Barthley			61				
3144	Conneely, Bartley '.			63				
74	Conneely, Beartla '.	c.1831		531	Honor 'Nora McDonagh	c.1861	5	1
64	Conneely, Brid '.	1866	c 1943	74	Patrick '. Conneely	c.1886-90	12	1
3139	Conneely, Bridget '.			63				
1126	Conneely, Bridget '.			61	Thomas Sullivan		3	1
81	Conneely, Christina			80				
79	Conneely, Coilin			61				
3143	Conneely, Colm '.			63				

An extract from the database of 2843 individuals (1 October 2013) including the Anglo-Norman Lynches who settled in Galway and members of my extended family (PaulBMcNulty.com on http://www.myfamily) (Ch = number of children; M = number of marriages).

Num	Name	Birth date	Died	Father	Spouse	Married	Ch	M
3124	Conneely, Edmond 'Ned'			65				
77	Conneely, James 'Jimi'			61				
3171	Conneely, John '.			61				
3142	Conneely, Johnny			63				
3138	Conneely, Laurence '.			63				
65	Conneely, Learai S.	c.1825	c.1893/c.68y	67	Barbara '. McDonagh	bef 1854	5	1
1133	Conneely, Mairin				Michael Sullivan	c 1998		1
3114	Conneely, Margaret			67				
3126	Conneely, Margaret			65				
3128	Conneely, Margaret '.			74				
181	Conneely, Margaret	c 1908		63	Michael McDonagh		1	1
3146	Conneely, Martin			63				
80	Conneely, Martin '.	25 Nov 1947	15 Jul 1977/29	61	Nuala Conneely		1	1
3129	Conneely, Martin '.			74				
1083	Conneely, Mary							
3145	Conneely, Mary			63				
3122	Conneely, Mary 'Maire			74	James Jos McDonough		1	1
3125	Conneely, Mary 'Maire'			65				
3116	Conneely, Matthew			67				
3140	Conneely, Nora			63				
82	Conneely, Nuala	c 1952			Martin '. Conneely		1	1
3130	Conneely, Patrick '.			74				
63	Conneely, Patrick '.	1855	c.1927-28/c.71	65	Brid '. Conneely	c.1886-90	12	1
61	Conneely, Patrick '.	25 Nov 1902	21 Jul 1985/82	63	Anne 'Nan McDonagh	c.1935	8	1
531	Conneely, Patrick '.	c 1795					1	1
3115	Conneely, Penelope '.			67				
3127	Conneely, Penelope '.			65				
3147	Conneely, Penelope '.			63				
18	Conneely, Treasa '.			61	Paul Bernard McNulty	21 Sep 1974	3	1
420	Connolly, ???				Nuala Walsh		1	1
3113	Connolly, Bridget	c.1866			Colman Walsh	c.1890	1	1
67	Connolly, John 'Sean	c.1792	c.1858/66y	417			4	1
417	Connolly, John Sean			420			1	1
1125	Connor, Mary							
1503	Constant, Guillemette				John 'Jean' Lynch	26 Nov 1709	4	1
1117	Conway, Catherine							
1118	Conway, John							
2843	Cooke, ???			2844			1	1
2844	Cooke, Barthly '.	1770	1850	2851	Mary Hynes		2	1
2669	Cooke, Bartholomew '.	1924		2566	Mary Ryan		1	1
2555	Cooke, Catherine '.			1447				
1444	Cooke, Ellen	c.1877	1953/76y	1445	Patrick Lynch	14 Aug 1902	6	1
2846	Cooke, James	1813	1882	2844	Kathleen '. Kelly		1	1
2848	Cooke, James 'Jamie'	1848	1922	2846	Mary Healy		1	1
2566	Cooke, John	1877	1953	2848	Mary O'Brien	c.1915	3	1
2851	Cooke, John						1	1
2553	Cooke, Joseph			1447	Margaret ZZ?			1
1447	Cooke, Michael J			1445	Margaret Gannon	c.1915	3	1
2567	Cooke, Michael John			2566	Martha Fleming	1964		1
2850	Cooke, Noel	1968		2669				
2671	Cooke, Pauline			2566	Dermot O'Neill			1
1449	Cooke, Terence J	1 Mar 1921	6 Oct 1983/62y	1447				
1445	Cooke, Thomas	1839	10 Feb 1899	2843	Catherine Rabbit		2	1
2557	Cooke, ZZ?				Nora Gannon			1
1959	Corbet, G						1	1
1958	Corbet, Victoire			1959	F. Lynch-Staunton	1857	2	1
91	Corcoran, Delia ? '.				Thomas Fallon			1
1689	Cormick, Richard W.				Lucy B. Staunton		1	1
1688	Cormick, Victoire	c 1771	aft 1810	1689	Marcus 'Mark' Lynch	Dec 1792	7	1
3077	Cory, Emily Vivian		21 Aug 1936		Francis Lynch-Blosse	15 Dec 1885	1	1
831	Cottle, Sibella				Henry Lynch-Blosse		7	1
2239	Counsell, Mariana Mary				Edward Martin	2 Dec 1862		1
3093	Courtney, ?			54	? Burke		1	1

Num	Name	Birth date	Died	Father	Spouse	Married	Ch	M
3098	Courtney, ?			54	? Lally			1
29	Courtney, Bridget	c 1846	2 Feb 1939	54	Patrick McHugh	3 Apr 1875	6	1
399	Courtney, W 'Cortney?'						1	1
54	Courtney, William	c 1812	c 1861/49y	399			3	1
1025	Cox, ???						3	1
1029	Cox, Breedhven			1025				
1027	Cox, Joseph R			1025	Frances ? Mooney			1
1023	Cox, Michael F (Dr)	1852	1926	1025	Dorothy? ZZ?		1	1
1531	Crean, Andrew	1705		2063	Mary Lynch	6 Jan 1751	4	1
2767	Crean, Arthur				Mary Lynch			1
2063	Crean, Henry	1670		2067	Catherine Blake	1703	1	1
2067	Crean, Stephen						1	1
1528	Crean-Lynch, Alice '.			1519	Francis Moffitt	1809-10		1
1537	Crean-Lynch, Andrew			1531				
782	Crean-Lynch, Andrew	10 Oct 1787		1519	Elizabeth Lynch	Jan 1811		1
1530	Crean-Lynch, Catherine			1519				
1519	Crean-Lynch, Dominick	1757	1806?	1531	Julia Browne	1784	6	2
1527	Crean-Lynch, Edward			1519				
1538	Crean-Lynch, Jane			1531	Martin Browne			1
1523	Crean-Lynch, Martin			1519	Charlotte Glanville			1
1535	Crean-Lynch, Mary		7 Dec 1807	1531	Thomas Dillon	c 1777		1
2523	Crean-Lynch, Patrick	c.1785		1519				
2530	Cresacre, Anne	1511	1577		John 'More' Moore		1	1
1200	Crowe, John						1	1
1196	Crowe, Julia	c 1881		1195				
1195	Crowe, Patrick	c 1832		1200	Mary Fallon	17 Dec 1877	2	1
1197	Crowe, Thomas	c 1883		1195				
56	Culkeen, Catherine	c 1823			James Fallon	5 Mar 1843	2	1
1088	Culkeen, Honor							
1087	Culkeen, Mark							
2700	Cullen, Elizabeth				Andrew Lynch			1
2696	Cullen, Thomas				Elizabeth Lynch			1
1219	Cullinane, ???						1	1
1236	Cullinane, John '.							
1234	Cullinane, Martin							
356	Cullinane, Mary	c 1802	12 Feb 1869	1219	John Fallon	c.1817	5	2
1233	Cullinane, Mrs							
1078	Cullinane, Walter '.							
2701	Cuniss, Barbara			2929	John Lynch		7	1
2929	Cuniss, Geoffrey '.						1	1
2245	Cunningham, Elizabeth	abt 1838			Richard Martin	9 Jul 1858		1
281	Cunningham, Mary	c.1837		2820	Michael O'Brien	4 Feb 1869	2	1
2820	Cunningham, Michael						1	1
2645	Curtis, Lily				Edward Whitby Lynch		2	1
2722	Cusack, Mary				Henry Lynch	c.1800		2
394	Cussen, Mary							
2590	Daly, Denis	c.1900		2588				
2588	Daly, Denis (Capt)		Nov 1899	2589	Kathleen Mary Lynch	3 Jun 1899	2	1
2769	Daly, Denise	c.1900		2588	William de Vere Cole	30 Sep 1918		1
2589	Daly, John Archer						1	1
2301	Darcy, ???				??? Kirwan		1	1
2749	Darcy, ???				Maurice Lynch	c.1701	2	1
2789	Darcy, ???				Ellen Lynch		1	1
916	Darcy, ???			619				
1559	Darcy, Anastacia			667	Dominick Browne		2	1
1858	Darcy, Anastacia '.			1859	Maurice Blake		3	1
2985	Darcy, Andrew		c.1650	667				
2264	Darcy, Anthony				Jennet Browne		1	1
1309	Darcy, Catherine			1311	Henry French	19 Feb 1628		2
1344	Darcy, Catherine			2264	Marcus French		2	1
1851	Darcy, Catherine				Hyacinth Darcy	bef 1716	3	1
1346	Darcy, Clare			1347	Edward Hamilton		1	1
2295	Darcy, Dominick			2872	Garrett '. Lynch			1

An extract from the database of 2843 individuals (1 October 2013) including the Anglo-Norman Lynches who settled in Galway and members of my extended family (PaulBMcNulty.com on http://www.myfamily) (Ch = number of children; M = number of marriages).

Num	Name	Birth date	Died	Father	Spouse	Married	Ch	M
2979	Darcy, Dominick		26 Dec 1727	2976	Elizabeth Butler		1	1
2982	Darcy, Dominick			2979	Bridget Blake			1
1653	Darcy, Elizabeth				1654 Michael (Capt) Lynch		2	1
2300	Darcy, Elizabeth		3 Jun 1636	2301	Hugh '. O'Flaherty	1626	1	2
949	Darcy, Frances				1850 Robert '. French	c.1715	2	1
2960	Darcy, Francis		1692	2251	Catherine Usher		1	1
1408	Darcy, Henrietta				1409 Anthony Lynch	10 Feb 1872	6	1
619	Darcy, Hyacinth				925 Mary Blake		2	2
921	Darcy, Hyacinth				817 Frances O'Brien		1	1
1850	Darcy, Hyacinth (Capt)	1665	1743	2960	Catherine Darcy	bef 1716	3	1
2383	Darcy, James	1633	1692	2251	Margaret '. Browne			1
2483	Darcy, James			1850	Jane Martin			1
667	Darcy, James 'Rivagh'		12 Jun 1603		Anastacia Bodkin		5	2
1347	Darcy, John						1	1
1859	Darcy, John						1	1
2790	Darcy, John			2789				
817	Darcy, John			1850	Jane Lynch		2	1
917	Darcy, John	26 Nov 1785		619	Frances Blake	4 Jun 1804		1
925	Darcy, John			817	Elizabeth ? Lynch	c.1752	1	2
2174	Darcy, Marcus						1	1
1311	Darcy, Martin		c.1636	667	Christian '. Martin		2	1
1597	Darcy, Martin							
1654	Darcy, Martin		17 Oct 1690	2868	Catherine Blake	20 May 1653	2	1
2173	Darcy, Mary			2174	James Martin			1
2872	Darcy, Nicholas			667			1	1
2203	Darcy, Patrick		2 Feb 1804	921	Mary Martin	4 Nov 1775		1
2251	Darcy, Patrick	1598	1668/70y	667	Mary French	1628	2	1
1409	Darcy, Richard						1	1
2155	Darcy, Richard				Anne Blake			1
2868	Darcy, Richard		bef 1656	1311	Mary Browne		1	1
2976	Darcy, Richard		16 Dec 1727	1654	Catherine Blake		1	1
1849	Davies, Elizabeth				Thomas Michel Lynch	c 1821		1
2609	Deane, ???				Andrew Lynch	1614	1	1
2933	Deane, Mary		1803		Dominick Skerrett		3	1
2968	Deaves, Anthony				Eleanor '. Lynch			1
3081	Delahaize, Dorothy		26 Oct 1962		Cecil Lynch-Blosse	31 Oct 1915	1	1
2959	Devenish, Christopher				Anne Lynch			1
1002	Dillon, Barbara				Christopher Bellew		3	1
1572	Dillon, Christopher	1760	1815		Margaret Lynch	10 Feb 1794		1
2475	Dillon, John						1	1
2474	Dillon, Rosa ?			2475	Thomas Lynch		1	1
1536	Dillon, Thomas		5 Feb 1801		Mary Crean-Lynch	c 1777		1
1812	Dinan, Alan 'de'						1	1
1811	Dinan, Gervase 'de'			1812	Richard Marshal	bef 1224		1
2803	Dodgworth, Luke				Mary Lynch	4 Jul 1807		1
1387	Doherty, John				Margaret Lynch			1
489	Dollard, Mary Kate	c 1894	c 1953		Patrick Fallon	1912	4	1
2913	Dolphin, George				Annabel '. Lynch	bef 1766		1
548	Donoghue, John	c 1855			Anne Burke		1	1
547	Donoghue, Mary Therese	c 1890		548	Stephen Glennon		1	1
554	Dooley, John	c 1860			Lena Burke	c 1905	1	1
555	Dooley, John			554	Claire Griffin			1
1673	Dowell, Frances			1674	C. Redington	Apr 1812	1	1
1674	Dowell, Henry						1	1
2534	Drake, Elizabeth				Winston Churchill		1	1
1573	Drouillard, Elizabeth			1847	Thomas Michel Lynch	May 1740	6	1
1847	Drouillard, Pierre						1	1
243	Duane, Anne	c 1798			John Farrell	2 Feb 1818	2	1
300	Duane?, John ?							
558	Duffy, Mary				Lawrence Griffin		1	1
459	Duffy, Mary 'Maura'				Patrick Fallon			1
1184	Duggan, Mary							
1965	Duncan, A S						1	1

An extract from the database of 2843 individuals (1 October 2013) including the Anglo-Norman Lynches who settled in Galway and members of my extended family (PaulBMcNulty.com on http://www.myfamily) (Ch = number of children; M = number of marriages).

Num	Name	Birth date	Died	Father	Spouse	Married	Ch	M
1964	Duncan, Marion			1965	R. Lynch-Staunton			1
2726	Eager, Francis (Capt)				Catherine Lynch			1
354	Egan, Marianne							
1807	Eleanor, Princess	1215		1808	William Marshal			1
2723	Elwood, John				Mary Cusack			1
2192	Evans, Harriet	c 1769	17 Sep 1846	2193	Robert Hesketh	5 Jun 1796	5	2
2193	Evans, Hugh	c 1743			Mary Manning		1	1
2796	Eyre, Jane				Martin (BL) Lynch			1
427	Fadden, Anna R							
401	Fahy, ???						1	1
312	Fahy, Honoria							
17	Fahy, Mary	c 1810		401	Charles O'Brien	c 1833	2	1
2739	Fair, Thomas				Margaret Lynch			1
1224	Fallon, ???						2	1
1228	Fallon, ???			1224	??? O'Connell		1	1
1246	Fallon, ???	c.1787-1804		479	??? Rushe		1	1
1249	Fallon, ???			479	??? Fox		2	1
2782	Fallon, Andrew			2781			1	1
446	Fallon, Anita			105				
1097	Fallon, Anne							
456	Fallon, Anne	c 1930		102	Frederick Alldritt			1
87	Fallon, Anne 'Annie'							
484	Fallon, Anne Mary	21 May 1900	31 Dec 1961	99				
449	Fallon, Anthony F							
3034	Fallon, Bernard						1	1
448	Fallon, Bridget '.							
1137	Fallon, Caroline	1950		490				1
1121	Fallon, Catherine							
1223	Fallon, Catherine	c 1868		1224				
357	Fallon, Catherine	c 1824	24 Nov 1884	355	Thomas Kearney	14 Aug 1847	15	1
440	Fallon, Catherine			105				
98	Fallon, Catherine	1869	c.1940/c.71y	14	John Joseph Fallon	2 Nov 1893	8	1
451	Fallon, Charles	May 1874		14	??? Collins			1
467	Fallon, Charles	c 1944		102	Madeleine Shanahan			1
491	Fallon, Charles			450				
2541	Fallon, Charles (Dr)							
1138	Fallon, Colette			490				1
443	Fallon, Conor			105				
1136	Fallon, Constance ?			490				
2781	Fallon, Cornelius '.		bef 1539				1	1
526	Fallon, Cressida			508				
523	Fallon, David			508				
1167	Fallon, Delia	1866		363				
525	Fallon, Dervilla			508				
493	Fallon, Eileen			450				
1180	Fallon, Elizabeth	1870		363				
1171	Fallon, Ellen	1867		363				
445	Fallon, Emer			105				
486	Fallon, Francis	c 1904		99				
1103	Fallon, Henry	1858	1902	363				
1172	Fallon, Henry							
1193	Fallon, Honor							
1163	Fallon, Honor '.	1865		363				
447	Fallon, James	1872	10 Jan 1948/75	14				
483	Fallon, James	5 Jul 1898	20 Aug 1947	99				
55	Fallon, James	1818		355	Catherine Culkeen	5 Mar 1843	2	1
2542	Fallon, James (Dr)							
479	Fallon, James ?		17 Sep 1826		??? Caulfield?		5	1
1120	Fallon, James J							
524	Fallon, Jessica			508				
1086	Fallon, John	1844	1844	55				
1100	Fallon, John							
1164	Fallon, John							

An extract from the database of 2843 individuals (1 October 2013) including the Anglo-Norman Lynches who settled in Galway and members of my extended family (PaulBMcNulty.com on http://www.myfamily) (Ch = number of children; M = number of marriages).

Num	Name	Birth date	Died	Father	Spouse	Married	Ch	M
14	Fallon, John	1845	28 May 1932	55	Anne O'Brien	26 Sep 1868	10	1
355	Fallon, John	c.1799	12 Apr 1827	479	Mary Cullinane	c.1817	5	1
454	Fallon, John	c 1929	2001?	102	Eileen McGarry		1	1
490	Fallon, John	1913	1969	450	Joan ZZ?	1948	3	1
506	Fallon, John	c 1857	8 May 1868/11y	363				
1284	Fallon, John 'O'				Joan 'Joanna' Lynch			1
1414	Fallon, John (BL)	c.1836		3034	Cecilia Lynch	19 Jul 1865		1
100	Fallon, John Henry	27 Oct 1896		99	Frances Glynn			1
99	Fallon, John Joseph	1869	22 Feb 1940/71	363	Catherine Fallon	2 Nov 1893	8	1
463	Fallon, Josephine	c 1939		102	Padraig Rigney			1
359	Fallon, Julia	c 1820	c 1885	355	John Morris	16 Jan 1842	3	1
2783	Fallon, Julia '.			2782	Donal O'Vulloghan	bef 1539		1
1106	Fallon, Julia Bedelia	1860		363				
462	Fallon, Julie Mai	c 1937		102				
444	Fallon, Kevin			105				
95	Fallon, Marion			93	Martin Forde		1	1
363	Fallon, Martin	1822	21 Apr 1892/71	355	Anne Boyle		9	1
368	Fallon, Martin	5 Sep 1894	1 Feb 1951	99	Mary Gillen	c.1942	1	1
522	Fallon, Martin			508				
86	Fallon, Martin							
508	Fallon, Martin '.	c 1944	15 Aug 1997/53	368	Phyllis Acton		5	1
93	Fallon, Martin 'Murt'	1880	c 1925	14	M Gilmore		1	1
1098	Fallon, Mary	1854	c 1938	363	Patrick Crowe	17 Dec 1877	2	1
1173	Fallon, Mary							
13	Fallon, Mary	23 Sep 1883	2 Aug 1950/66y	14	Thomas McHugh	7 Jan 1909	7	1
482	Fallon, Mary	1870	c 1871	14				
383	Fallon, Mary Kate '.	c.1912	15 Jul 1987/75	99				
102	Fallon, Michael	c.1875	28 Apr 1964/89	14	Winifred Greaney	c.1921	10	2
3102	Fallon, Michael			454				
441	Fallon, Michael			105				
460	Fallon, Michael '.	c 1934		102	Maureen Luby			1
1202	Fallon, Patrick						1	1
1207	Fallon, Patrick		2 Jul 1927	1211	Anne '. McDonagh	6 Jun 1895		1
1211	Fallon, Patrick		bef 1895				1	1
1232	Fallon, Patrick							
450	Fallon, Patrick	1879	1970	14	Mary Kate Dollard	1912	4	1
458	Fallon, Patrick	c 1932		102	Mary 'Maura' Duffy			1
481	Fallon, Patrick	1805	13 May 1879	479				
1165	Fallon, Sarah	c.1859	c.1944/c.85y	1202	Thomas Greaney	28 Feb 1878	4	1
465	Fallon, Seamus	c 1940		102	Christobel McArthur			1
105	Fallon, Thomas	1935		102	Mary Walsh	1972	7	1
442	Fallon, Thomas			105				
485	Fallon, Thomas	c 1902		99				
89	Fallon, Thomas	1877	23 Jun 1970/96	14	Mary A '. O'Malley			2
505	Fallon, Thomas (Rev)	c.1786	13 Mar 1839	479				
469	Fallon, Una	c 1942		102	Victor Feldman	c.1965		1
487	Fallon, Una	c 1908		99				
361	Fallon, Winifred	c 1826		355	??? ? McCormack			1
492	Fallon, Winifred			450				
92	Fallon, Winifred (Sr	21 Oct 1885	c.1970	14				
206	Fanelli, Robert S				Maureen H Harrigan	c 1962		1
246	Farrell, ???				Mary ZZ?	c 1785	1	1
310	Farrell, Anne	1865		236				
304	Farrell, Bridget	c 1860		236				
528	Farrell, Catherine	c 1879		236				
311	Farrell, James			236				
527	Farrell, James	c 1876		236				
242	Farrell, John	c 1789	10 Nov 1859/72	246	Anne Duane	2 Feb 1818	2	1
244	Farrell, John	c 1821		242				
253	Farrell, John	c 1913		235				
2836	Farrell, John				Anastacia '. Lynch			1
235	Farrell, John 'Jack' P	20 May 1868	26 Oct 1955/83	236	Margaret Ryan	21 Feb 1906	4	1
217	Farrell, Martin	11 Nov 1911	3 Aug 1996/84y	235	Mary 'Mai' Griffin	28 Nov 1956	1	1

An extract from the database of 2843 individuals (1 October 2013) including the Anglo-Norman Lynches who settled in Galway and members of my extended family (PaulBMcNulty.com on http://www.myfamily) (Ch = number of children; M = number of marriages).

Num	Name	Birth date	Died	Father	Spouse	Married	Ch	M
175	Farrell, Mary			217	Kieran McHugh	26 Jun 1999	4	1
307	Farrell, Mary	1862		236				
251	Farrell, Mary Ann	c 1907		235	Michael Monaghan		3	1
308	Farrell, Michael							
1385	Farrell, Patrick				Joan 'Joanna' Lynch			1
252	Farrell, Patrick	c 1909	c.1993	235	Mary? ZZ?			1
236	Farrell, Patrick '.	1819	c.1890/c.71y	242	Catherine Flynn	c.1860	6	1
303	Farrell, Winifred							
470	Feldman, Victor				Una Fallon	c.1965		1
1836	Ferrers, William		1254		Sibilla Marshal	bef 1219		1
2591	Field, Eliza Mgt? C.				Peter Lynch	c.1740	7	1
2652	Filmer, Harry				Helen Lynch			1
518	Finn, Ann				Francis '. Kearney	10 Sep 1977	2	1
373	Finn, Bridget				Lawrence Griffin		2	1
1170	Finn, Kate ?							
1179	Finn, Mary ?							
1169	Finn, Michael ?							
1870	Finnis, Elizabeth	21 Apr 1785	12 Mar 1845/60	1871	Henry (Major) Lynch	1800	11	1
1871	Finnis, Robert						1	1
1360	Fitzgerald, Edward			1359				
2409	Fitzgerald, Eleanor				Murrough O'Brien		1	1
1362	Fitzgerald, Francis			1359				
1361	Fitzgerald, John			1359				
2408	Fitzgerald, Margaret				Peter 'Piers' Butler		1	1
1359	Fitzgerald, Patrick				Julia Burke		3	1
2231	Fitzpatrick, Edmond				Annabel '. Martin		1	1
2387	Fitzpatrick, Richard		1761	2231				
73	Flaherty, Honor	c.1834		535	Martin '. McDonagh	2 Nov 1856	1	1
2633	Flanagan, John						1	1
2632	Flanagan, Marcella		8 Sep 1831	2633	Patrick Lynch	1820	2	1
779	Fleeson, Anna Maria			1514	Peter Gale?			2
1514	Fleeson, Plunket						1	1
2568	Fleming, Martha				Michael John Cooke	1964		1
714	Fleming, Simona			715	William ? U. Lynch		2	1
715	Fleming, Thomas						1	1
351	Flynn, ???	c 1800			??? Broderick?	c 1830	1	1
237	Flynn, Catherine	c.1845	c.1905/c.60y	351	Patrick '. Farrell	c.1860	6	1
309	Flynn, Mary							
1158	Flynn, Michael				Maureen Kearney			1
700	Font, ???			1258	Geoffrey W. Lynch		2	1
2150	Font, Adam				Julia '. Blake			1
1258	Font, Walter						1	1
97	Forde, Desmond 'Des'			96				
96	Forde, Martin				Marion Fallon		1	1
1183	Forde, Michael							
1932	Foster, ? (Major)				Anne 'Anna V. Lynch			1
1251	Fox, ? (Mother M.			1250				
1254	Fox, ? (Mother Mary	c 1865	1 May 1958/93y	1252				
1250	Fox, ???				??? Fallon		2	1
1252	Fox, ???			1250			1	1
997	Francis, Gordon Hamer						1	1
996	Francis, Jacqueline			997	Richard Lynch-Blosse	27 May 2000		1
1943	French, ???						2	1
2602	French, ???				H?? Lynch		1	1
2611	French, ???				Henry Lynch	1644	1	1
2987	French, ???						2	1
594	French, Andrew				Reddith Lynch			1
1942	French, Anne			1943	Patrick Lynch	1747	2	1
2169	French, Anthony						1	1
2444	French, Arthur				Julia Lynch			1
2575	French, Arthur		1753		Joan Lynch		2	1
1272	French, Catherine				William Lynch		1	1
1340	French, Catherine			1341	Darcy Hamilton		1	1

An extract from the database of 2843 individuals (1 October 2013) including the Anglo-Norman Lynches who settled in Galway and members of my extended family (PaulBMcNulty.com on http://www.myfamily) (Ch = number of children; M = number of marriages).

Num	Name	Birth date	Died	Father	Spouse	Married	Ch	M
2221	French, Catherine	c 1661		2222	Richard '. Martin	c 1681	8	1
2329	French, Cecilia			2330	Brian B. O'Flaherty	Apr 1707	1	1
1945	French, Charles (Bt)			1943				
2876	French, Christopher		1688	2874	Margaret Blake	1 Nov 1686		1
2032	French, Eleanor				Philip Lynch Athy		4	1
730	French, Ellis			731	Robert '. Lynch	aft Apr 162	13	1
2504	French, Eveline			2505	Valentine Blake		1	1
2750	French, Francis			2575	Julia Lynch	2 Sep 1771		1
2505	French, Geoffrey						1	1
1310	French, Henry		aft 1641		Catherine Darcy	19 Feb 1628		1
2880	French, Hyacinth		c.1748	1852	Surna Blake	22 Mar 1703	1	1
2330	French, James						1	1
2168	French, Jane				2169 Nicholas Martin			1
1323	French, Joan				1324 Martin Lynch	19 Apr 1702	6	1
735	French, Joan 'Jennet'				731 Maurice '. Lynch	c.1632	1	1
2268	French, Joan 'Jennett'				2269 Anthony Lynch		13	1
1497	French, John						1	1
3049	French, John				Ellis Lynch			1
1343	French, Marcus		c 1691	2262	Catherine Darcy		2	1
955	French, Marcus		16 May 1719	1341	Ann Hamilton	1694		2
1496	French, Margaret				1497 Thomas Lynch		2	1
2146	French, Margaret				2147 Valentine (1st Blake		5	1
2249	French, Margaret				731 Richard Martin		1	1
2577	French, Margaret	c.1751			2575 Charles Lynch		5	1
1366	French, Mary				Walter Burke			1
2250	French, Mary			731	Peter Blake		2	2
2438	French, Mary				Marcus Lynch	28 Jul 1679	1	1
2971	French, Mary				Arthur Lynch			1
950	French, Mary			948	Martin Kirwan			2
2112	French, Mary 'Maria'		1694	1343	Thomas (4th Blake	6 Oct 1656		1
1587	French, Mary 'Marie'				John 'Jean' Lynch		9	1
1728	French, Mary ?				Dominick Lynch		5	1
2269	French, Nicholas						1	1
1604	French, Patrick				Monique Lynch	1774		1
1852	French, Patrick		5 Jun 1708	2874	??? Blake		2	2
946	French, Patrick		c.1767	2880	Catherine Skerrett		1	1
2262	French, Patrick fitz		6 Feb 1630		Mary Kirwan		1	1
731	French, Peter (Sir)		27 Feb 1631		Mary Browne		4	1
1324	French, Peter fitz H.						1	1
2147	French, Robert '.						1	1
2222	French, Robert '.						1	1
2874	French, Robert '.		Apr 1691		Christina '. ZZ?		2	1
948	French, Robert '.			1852	Frances Darcy	c.1715	2	1
1341	French, Robert (Capt)		aft 1700	1343	Mary Lambert		2	1
938	French, Sibilla			948	Maurice Blake	c.1733	2	1
945	French, Surna		1790	946	Marcus Lynch	2 Jan 1767		1
2988	French, Thomas			2987				
2297	French, Valentine				Mary Lynch			1
2527	Gage, Elizabeth	1585	1610		Cresacre '. Moore		1	1
1614	Galayn, Rosa de la C.				Patrick '. Lynch	1749	1	1
1518	Gale?, Peter				Anna Maria Fleeson			1
2551	Gannon, ???						3	1
2550	Gannon, Margaret		1930	2551	Michael J Cooke	c.1915	3	1
2552	Gannon, Mary			2551				
2556	Gannon, Nora	c.1877		2551	ZZ? Cooke			1
3008	Garvey, ???				Mary Moore			1
1635	Gedea, Hilda				Che 'de la Guevara	c 1954		1
1908	Geoghegan, ??? (Lt C.				Barbara Lynch	1851		1
1160	Giblin, Bartholomew				Winifred Kearney			1
866	Gibson, Catherine				Henry Blake		1	1
39	Gillen, Emer				Hugh McNulty	27 Dec 1980	2	1
507	Gillen, Mary	c 1917			Martin Fallon	c.1942	1	1
94	Gilmore, M				Martin 'Murt' Fallon		1	1

An extract from the database of 2843 individuals (1 October 2013) including the Anglo-Norman Lynches who settled in Galway and members of my extended family (PaulBMcNulty.com on http://www.myfamily) (Ch = number of children; M = number of marriages).

Num	Name	Birth date	Died	Father	Spouse	Married	Ch	M
1525	Glanville, ??? (Chief						1	1
1524	Glanville, Charlotte			1525	Martin Crean-Lynch			1
545	Glennon, Maureen	c.1920		546	Joseph Griffin			1
546	Glennon, Stephen	c 1885			Mary T. Donoghue		1	1
171	Gloster, Christabel				John McHugh	c 1987	2	1
101	Glynn, Frances				John Henry Fallon			1
1238	Goary?, Mary							
2994	Golding, ???				Mary Lynch			1
3070	Gore, Anne				John (Ld A. Browne	Dec 1729	2	1
2901	Gorman, Anne			845				
844	Gorman, Elizabeth			845	Robert Lynch-Blosse	8 Sep 1800	5	1
845	Gorman, John? William?						3	1
2902	Gorman, Martha			845				
2656	Gowthorpe, John			2655				
2655	Gowthorpe, Roy				Sybil Lynch	1918	1	1
1925	Grace, Helen				George A Williams			2
2056	Gradwell, Annette F.			2057	Edmond J P Athy	25 Oct 1881	1	1
2057	Gradwell, Richard						1	1
3015	Graham, Emily G.		10 May 1962	3016	Henry (Col) Lynch	16 Jun 1898	1	1
3016	Graham, Ogilvie Blair						1	1
498	Grealish, ???						1	1
1187	Grealish, Bridget							
500	Grealish, James	c 1899		471				
1109	Grealish, John							
501	Grealish, John	c 1900	16 Oct 1961	471			1	1
1198	Grealish, Martin							
1073	Grealish, Mary	1879		473				
1110	Grealish, Mary							
1072	Grealish, Mary Mgt '.	1877		473				
1111	Grealish, Michael	c.1862		473				
1112	Grealish, Michael							
471	Grealish, Patrick	1860	23 May 1951	473	Julia Jennings	31 Jan 1898	3	1
473	Grealish, Patrick	c 1833	1917/84y	498	Mary McGuire	29 Jan 1855	8	1
1168	Grealish, Peter	1867		473				
1077	Grealish, Rodger	1869	31 Jul 1891/21	473				
1178	Grealish, Rodger '.							
1075	Grealish, Rodger (Fr)	c.1947	31 Jul 1986/39	501				
1071	Grealish, William	1874		473				
104	Grealish, Winifred	9 Dec 1903	27 Apr 1983/79	471	Michael Fallon	3 Nov 1927	10	1
1076	Grealish, Winifred	1871	28 Mar 1900/27	473				
1222	Greaney, Molly '.	1891		1188				
1221	Greaney, Nora	c 1889		1188				
1191	Greaney, Patrick	1881		1188				
1190	Greaney, Sarah							
1181	Greaney, Thomas							
1188	Greaney, Thomas	c 1841	c 1897	1205	Sarah Fallon	28 Feb 1878	4	1
509	Greaney, Thomas	c 1853			Bridget ZZ?	c 1888	1	1
1185	Greaney, Walter							
1189	Greaney, William	1879	c.1952/c.73y	1188				
1205	Greaney, William		c 1863				1	1
103	Greaney, Winifred	c.1892	c.1924/c.32y	509	Michael Fallon	c.1921		1
1182	Greaney, Winifred							
428	Greavey, Honoria		14 Feb 1934		Michael Walsh	8 Apr 1916		1
639	Grehan, Elizabeth '.	c 1816	1857/41y	640	Nicholas Lynch	24 Nov 1835	3	1
640	Grehan, Stephen				Margaret Ryan		1	1
377	Griffin, ? 'Ciss'	c 1890	c 1905	370				
270	Griffin, Andrew ? (Fr)	c 1832						
241	Griffin, Andrew C.	c 1888		232			1	1
378	Griffin, Annie	c 1894		370	Bartholomew Mason			1
559	Griffin, Claire	c 1940		375	John Dooley			1
561	Griffin, Helen			266	??? Keane			1
374	Griffin, John			372				
544	Griffin, Joseph	c.1915		241	Maureen Glennon			1

An extract from the database of 2843 individuals (1 October 2013) including the Anglo-Norman Lynches who settled in Galway and members of my extended family (PaulBMcNulty.com on http://www.myfamily) (Ch = number of children; M = number of marriages).

Num	Name	Birth date	Died	Father	Spouse	Married	Ch	M
250	Griffin, Josephine	c 1921		224				
248	Griffin, Kathleen	c 1917		224				
372	Griffin, Lawrence				Bridget Finn		2	1
375	Griffin, Lawrence	c 1886		370	Mary Duffy		1	1
267	Griffin, Mary	c 1864		264				
218	Griffin, Mary 'Mai'	1914		224	Martin Farrell	28 Nov 1956	1	1
263	Griffin, Mary Kate	c 1891	c 1896/5y	232				
249	Griffin, Maude	c 1919		224				
224	Griffin, Michael	c 1890		232	Bridget '. Leahy	c 1909	5	1
264	Griffin, Michael	c 1830			??? Bermingham		3	1
266	Griffin, Michael	c 1862		264			1	1
560	Griffin, Michael J.	18 Sep 1892	15 Nov 1920	370				
247	Griffin, Patrick	c 1916		224				
376	Griffin, Patrick	c 1888		370				
232	Griffin, Patrick ?	c.1860	c.1901-11	264	Mary 'Maria' Leahy	c.1886	3	1
370	Griffin, Thomas			372	Mary Kyne	5 Jul 1884	5	1
2241	Gubbins, Sarah	abt 1854			John Robert Martin	31 Aug 1874		1
1625	Guevara, Che 'de la	14 Jun 1928	9 Oct 1967	1623	Hilda Gedea	c 1954		2
1623	Guevara, Ernesto '.	1900	1990	1622	Celia y de la Serna	1927	1	1
1622	Guevara, Roberto '.				Ana 'y Ortiz' Lynch	1884	1	1
2603	Hackett, ???				Henry Ffrench Lynch			1
2217	Hall, Rebecca Hyde				John (Sir) Peshall		1	1
2255	Hamilton, Ann		bef 1709	2256	John Blake			2
1339	Hamilton, Darcy			1345	Catherine French		1	1
1345	Hamilton, Edward				Clare Darcy		1	1
1338	Hamilton, Julia			1339	Thomas Lynch	11 Feb 1740	2	1
2256	Hamilton, William						1	1
2939	Hanly, James				Catherine Lynch			1
1199	Hanly, Julia							
930	Hardinge, Robert N.				Mary Lynch-Blosse	8 Mar 1892		1
1954	Hardwick, Francis						1	1
1953	Hardwick, Sarah Jane			1954	G. Lynch-Staunton	1824	10	1
205	Harrigan, Maureen H	c 1937		119	Robert S Fanelli	c 1962		1
207	Harrigan, Thomas D	c 1939		119				
119	Harrigan, Thomas L				Mary Agnes McHugh	c 1935	2	1
184	Harte, Mary				John McDonagh		2	1
262	Hawkins, ???				Michael Smyth	c.1840	3	1
2849	Healy, Mary				James 'Jamie' Cooke		1	1
516	Heaney, Anne 'Annie'	12 Jan 1918	10 Jul 2003		John '. Kearney	11 Feb 1946	1	1
285	Heffernan, Molly				William O'Brien			1
405	Hendrick, ???						1	1
404	Hendrick, Julia			405	Joseph Bolger	c 1927	1	1
1810	Henry, King III			1808				
2194	Hesketh, Robert		1795		Harriet Evans	5 Jun 1796		1
2621	Hevey, Catherine			2622	Henry Lynch		5	1
2622	Hevey, Gerald						1	1
125	Higgins, Bridget '.	26 Jul 1916		88	Patrick '. Lynch	15 Apr 1948	7	1
131	Higgins, Nora	c 1917	c.15 Aug 1996	88				
132	Higgins, Patrick	c.1919	c.1921	88				
805	Higgins, Philip				Anne Lynch			1
88	Higgins, Thomas		c 1955		Mary McHugh		3	1
1113	Holland, Margaret							
2755	Hopkins, ???				Harriet Lynch			1
432	Horan, James							
3021	Horsley, Janet Duveen				Henry (Major) Lynch	14 Oct 1966	4	1
2054	Hounsell, Frederick				Mary Elizabeth Athy	28 Apr 1889	1	1
2055	Hounsell, Randle	1 Mar 1890		2054				
116	Hubbard, John				Martha T McHugh	c 1962		1
1744	Hubert, Sheila 'Shyly				Dermot O'Shaughnessy		2	1
984	Hudson, Charles W.						1	1
983	Hudson, Evangeline Mgt			984	Hely Lynch-Blosse	25 Apr 1922	1	1
142	Hughes, ???				Peter McHugh			1
2953	Hunt, ??? de Vere				Catherine Lynch			1

An extract from the database of 2843 individuals (1 October 2013) including the Anglo-Norman Lynches who settled in Galway and members of my extended family (PaulBMcNulty.com on http://www.myfamily) (Ch = number of children; M = number of marriages).

Num	Name	Birth date	Died	Father	Spouse	Married	Ch	M
1377	Hynes, ???				Catherine Burke			1
2692	Hynes, Catherine				Jonathan Lynch		4	1
2845	Hynes, Mary	1787	1850		Barthly '. Cooke		2	1
2097	Irvine, ???				Robert (Capt) Lynch			1
728	Jacob, Anne			723				
725	Jacob, Arthur			723				
726	Jacob, Francis			723				
727	Jacob, Mary			723				
724	Jacob, Robert			723				
723	Jacob, Robert (Sir)				Mary Lynch		5	1
496	Jennings, ???						1	1
472	Jennings, Julia	c 1868	16 Apr 1942/74	494	Patrick Grealish	31 Jan 1898	3	1
494	Jennings, Patrick		bef 1898	496			1	1
1808	John, King						2	1
3066	Johns, Moira Jean				Gerald Lynch-Blosse		2	1
2716	Jordan, Henry Dexter						1	1
2715	Jordan, Honoria			2716	Thomas Lynch		1	1
1659	Joyce, ??? 'Joyes'				Joseph Lynch		1	1
2014	Joyce, Anastacia			2015	Andrew (Capt) Athy		1	1
2493	Joyce, Andrew 'Joyes'						1	1
1647	Joyce, Anna 'Joyes'			1649	Henry 'Joyes' Joyce		2	2
1487	Joyce, Anne			1488	Andrew Lynch		4	1
1319	Joyce, Anne 'Anna J.		osp	1320	Thomas Lynch	9 Jan 1691		1
2015	Joyce, Dominick				Magdalene '. Lynch		2	1
2689	Joyce, Ellen			2687	??? (Dr) Kelly			1
2743	Joyce, Helena		1847	2744	Charles Lynch		2	1
1683	Joyce, Henrietta K.			1899	Thomas D W. Lynch	1901	2	1
1648	Joyce, Henry 'Joyes'				Anna 'Joyes' Joyce		1	1
514	Joyce, Honora	c.1877	23 Mar 1949		John Stephen Kearney	16 Jan 1902	1	1
2636	Joyce, James				Mary Lynch		1	1
2635	Joyce, Jane			2636	Henry Lynch	1860	1	1
2688	Joyce, John			2687				
1320	Joyce, John 'Joyes'			2493			2	1
1649	Joyce, Marcus 'Joyes'				Anna Bodkin		1	1
2793	Joyce, Maria			2015	Oliver Ormsby		2	1
1327	Joyce, Oliver 'Joyes'		c.1741	1320	Mary Lynch	c.1695		1
2687	Joyce, Patrick				Mary Lynch		2	1
1488	Joyce, Peter						1	1
1899	Joyce, Pierce John						1	1
1667	Joyce, Robert 'Joyes'			1648				
2744	Joyce, Walter						1	1
3134	Kacin, Richard '.				Mary McDonough			1
391	Kavanagh, ???	c 1780					1	1
60	Kavanagh, James	c 1810		391	Margaret ZZ?		1	1
25	Kavanagh, Margaret	c.1838	1 Mar 1890/51y	60	John Boylan	c.1861	6	1
562	Keane, ???				Helen Griffin			1
520	Kearney, Aisling			517				
1116	Kearney, Bedelia							
1105	Kearney, Bridget							
1145	Kearney, Bridget '.	1849		358	Patrick Smyth	c.1875	1	1
1153	Kearney, Catherine		2 Feb 1937	358	John '. Callanan			1
519	Kearney, Fiona	1 Oct 1982		517				
517	Kearney, Francis '.			515	Ann Finn	10 Sep 1977	2	1
1176	Kearney, Honor '.							
1101	Kearney, Honor 'Nora'	1857	1894	358	John Kearns			1
1174	Kearney, James	1868		358				
1093	Kearney, John	1852	bef 1859	358				
1175	Kearney, John							
515	Kearney, John '.	16 May 1906	26 Jul 1962/56	513	Anne 'Annie' Heaney	11 Feb 1946	1	1
513	Kearney, John Stephen	1858	6 Mar 1923/64y	358	Honora Joyce	16 Jan 1902	1	2
1161	Kearney, Joseph	1868	24 May 1903	358				
1108	Kearney, Julia	June 1860	1933	358	Owen Kerins			1
512	Kearney, Martin	1854	31 Oct 1886/31	358				

An extract from the database of 2843 individuals (1 October 2013) including the Anglo-Norman Lynches who settled in Galway and members of my extended family (PaulBMcNulty.com on http://www.myfamily) (Ch = number of children; M = number of marriages).

Num	Name	Birth date	Died	Father	Spouse	Married	Ch	M
1102	Kearney, Mary							
1143	Kearney, Mary Teresa	c.1848	10 Dec 1904	358	Patrick Whelan			1
1157	Kearney, Maureen			1155	Michael Flynn			1
1094	Kearney, Patrick							
511	Kearney, Patrick	c 1853	19 Oct 1906	358	Bridget Ryan			1
1155	Kearney, Richard	1865	12 Jan 1929	358	Catherine Ryan		1	1
1115	Kearney, Thomas							
1148	Kearney, Thomas	c.1855	24 Dec 1914	358	Margaret Collins			1
358	Kearney, Thomas	c 1817	12 Sep 1878		Catherine Fallon	14 Aug 1847	15	1
1114	Kearney, William	c.1864		358				
1159	Kearney, Winifred	1867	19 Feb 1941	358	Bartholomew Giblin			1
1095	Kearney?, Honor							
1150	Kearns, John				Honor 'Nora' Kearney			1
2682	Kelly, ???						2	1
2683	Kelly, ???			2682	James Lynch		3	1
3040	Kelly, ???				??? Lynch		1	1
2690	Kelly, ??? (Dr)				Ellen Joyce			1
1598	Kelly, Antoine							
2788	Kelly, Crofton			2787				
2787	Kelly, Edmond ?		aft 1749				2	1
785	Kelly, James						1	1
2674	Kelly, Jane			2682	Patrick Lynch		4	1
2785	Kelly, Jane			2787	Marcus 'Mark' Lynch	c.1747	1	1
2906	Kelly, John				Mary 'Molly' Lynch	c.1751		1
2847	Kelly, Kathleen 'Katy'				James Cooke		1	1
2180	Kelly, Mable 'Sweet'				Richard Martin			1
784	Kelly, Sarah			785	Patrick Lynch	1810	1	1
319	Kennedy, Catherine							
318	Kennedy, Francis							
322	Kennedy, Mary							
324	Kennedy, Michael							
321	Kennedy, Patrick '.							
317	Kennedy, Sara 'Sally'				John 'Lahy' Leahy		6	1
326	Kennedy, Thomas							
1152	Kerins, Owen		1897		Julia Kearney			1
1241	Kieran, John C							
3158	Kilkelly, ???				Nina Louisa Moore		1	1
3159	Kilkenny, Ethel			3158	ZZ? Reardon		2	1
2795	Killikelly, Bryan B.				Rebecca Ormsby			1
1995	Killikelly, Catherine			1996	George Moore	c 1765	3	1
1996	Killikelly, Dominick				Helen O'Kelly		1	1
1922	Kirkpatrick, James						1	1
1921	Kirkpatrick, Margaret			1922	G. Lynch-Staunton	1870	1	1
2302	Kirwan, ???				??? Darcy		1	1
1605	Kirwan, Abbe							
2178	Kirwan, Bridget	c 1688	bef May 1761	2218	Anthony Martin	c 1707	4	1
934	Kirwan, Christian			935	Marcus 'Mark' Blake	c.1777	1	1
943	Kirwan, Edmond						1	1
2191	Kirwan, Emily Sylvia				Richard (Rev) Martin	6 Dec 1821	7	1
2798	Kirwan, Joseph				Mary 'Maria' Lynch	24 Nov 1800		1
2212	Kirwan, Julia	c 1795	1858	2213	Thomas B (MP) Martin	14 Feb 1814	1	1
942	Kirwan, Julia			943	Marcus 'Mark' Blake	c.1712	2	1
2866	Kirwan, Julia '.				Martin (BL) Lynch			1
2218	Kirwan, Martin						1	1
935	Kirwan, Martin				Mary French		1	2
1638	Kirwan, Mary				Peter Lynch		1	1
2061	Kirwan, Mary				David John Wilson			1
2263	Kirwan, Mary				Patrick fitz French		1	1
2615	Kirwan, Mary				Henry Lynch	1703	1	1
1586	Kirwan, Michel David				Jane Jeanne Lynch			1
2213	Kirwan, Patrick	c.1769	bef 1814		Mary Burke		1	1
2224	Kirwan, Patrick				Mary Martin	c.1703		1
2500	Kirwan, Patrick				Jane Browne			1

An extract from the database of 2843 individuals (1 October 2013) including the Anglo-Norman Lynches who settled in Galway and members of my extended family (PaulBMcNulty.com on http://www.myfamily) (Ch = number of children; M = number of marriages).

Num	Name	Birth date	Died	Father	Spouse	Married	Ch	M
1729	Kirwan, Patrick fitz							
1261	Kirwan, William				Anastacia Lynch			1
960	Knight, Charlotte F.		1 May 1892	961	Henry Lynch-Blosse	16 Jul 1844	4	1
961	Knight, Robert (Rev)						1	1
3167	Kramer, ZZ?				Michelle Reardon			1
112	Kunsemuller, Dorothy		1989		Patrick H McHugh	3 Jul 1933	3	1
371	Kyne, Mary				Thomas Griffin	5 Jul 1884	5	1
2201	l'Espinasse, Jean P.						1	1
2200	l'Espinasse, Marie '.			2201	Anthony C. Martin	5 Oct 1806		1
1820	Lacy, John 'de'				Margaret 'de' Quenci		1	1
1834	Lacy, Maud 'de'			1820	Richard 'de' Clare			1
3099	Lally, ?				? Courtney			1
718	Lambert, Elizabeth			719	Nicholas Lynch		1	1
2260	Lambert, John		1683		Redish Lynch		1	1
2259	Lambert, Mary			2260	Robert (Capt) French		2	1
719	Lambert, Walter						1	1
149	Landy, John (Jack)	12 Jun 1916			Evelyn 'Eva' McHugh	19 Mar 1977		1
1815	Lanvallei, Margaret				Gilbert Marshal	Sep 1230		1
3064	Laughrane, Beatrice				Patrick Lynch-Blosse			1
1576	Le Berthon, Marie C.				John 'Jean B. Lynch		1	1
225	Leahy, Bridget '.	c 1885		226	Michael Griffin	c 1909	5	1
330	Leahy, Bridget 'Lahey'	17 Jun 1851		271				
323	Leahy, Bridget 'Lahy'	21 Jan 1821		316				
328	Leahy, Dennis 'Lahy'	18 Nov 1824		316				
226	Leahy, John	c.1849	c.1923/c.74y	256	Catherine '. Smyth	20 Feb 1882	5	1
230	Leahy, John	c.1891	young	226				
271	Leahy, John 'Lahey'	c 1820			Mary 'Maria' Coen	c 1847	8	1
341	Leahy, John 'Lahey'	11 Sep 1861		271				
256	Leahy, John 'Lahy'	14 Sep 1816		316			1	1
316	Leahy, John 'Lahy'				Sara 'Sally' Kennedy		6	1
320	Leahy, Judy? 'Lahy'	7 Mar 1819		316				
343	Leahy, Margaret '.	20 Nov 1863		271				
335	Leahy, Martin 'Lahey'	27 Jul 1854		271				
329	Leahy, Martin 'Lahy'	18 Nov 1824		316				
345	Leahy, Mary 'Maria L.							
233	Leahy, Mary 'Maria'	c.1849	aft 1910	271	Patrick ? Griffin	c.1886	3	1
229	Leahy, Mary Anne	c.1887		226				
228	Leahy, Michael '.	c 1883		226				
338	Leahy, Michael 'Lahey'	16 Aug 1856		271				
347	Leahy, Michael 'Lahy'							
231	Leahy, Patrick 'Paddy'	c 1896		226				
346	Leahy, Patrick Joseph	3 Jun 1866		271				
333	Leahy, Thomas 'Lahey'	28 Apr 1853		271				
325	Leahy, Thomas 'Lahy'	14 Mar 1823		316				
344	Leahy, Thomas 'Lahy'							
1711	Leonard, John						1	1
1692	Leonard, Margaret		1 Oct 1784	1711	George Staunton		2	1
2100	Leonard, Mary			2101	Thomas Lynch	30 Jul 1841		1
2101	Leonard, Stephen John						1	1
1213	Leonard, Tobias							
2818	Lewen, Anne			2819	Michael Lynch	27 Oct 1851		1
2819	Lewen, James (Capt)						1	1
1417	Lillias, Margaret				Anthony Lynch	23 Apr 1903		1
2582	Livesay, Charlotte			2583	Charles Lynch		2	1
2583	Livesay, Richard						1	1
1124	Long, Patrick							
1131	Long, Peter				Barbara Sullivan	c 2003		1
461	Luby, Maureen				Michael '. Fallon			1
1762	Lynch, ?			1262			1	1
1764	Lynch, ?			1762			2	1
1550	Lynch, ???			1533	Thomas Trench			1
2378	Lynch, ???			1277			1	1
2379	Lynch, ???			2378			1	1

An extract from the database of 2843 individuals (1 October 2013) including the Anglo-Norman Lynches who settled in Galway and members of my extended family (PaulBMcNulty.com on http://www.myfamily) (Ch = number of children; M = number of marriages).

Num	Name	Birth date	Died	Father	Spouse	Married	Ch	M
2461	Lynch, ???				??? Bodkin		1	1
2613	Lynch, ???				Andrew Lynch	1672	1	1
2704	Lynch, ???			2593	James McDonnell			1
2752	Lynch, ???			1567				
2762	Lynch, ???			2758				
2779	Lynch, ???			2778			1	1
2822	Lynch, ???				Elinor Bodkin		1	1
2917	Lynch, ???		bef 1762		Margaret Browne			1
2973	Lynch, ???						2	1
3039	Lynch, ???			620	??? Kelly		1	1
3073	Lynch, ???			3040				
808	Lynch, ???			858				1
1707	Lynch, Agnes			1611				
1778	Lynch, Agnes			1275				
2804	Lynch, Agnes				Joseph Barradaele	8 Nov 1817		1
2839	Lynch, Agnes			2830				
2911	Lynch, Agnes		bef Feb 1761	2912				
702	Lynch, Agnes			1286	James Lynch		1	1
1500	Lynch, Alexander			1486				
1781	Lynch, Alexander	c 1719	1799/80y	1780			2	1
884	Lynch, Alexander			693				
1504	Lynch, Alexander (Rev)			1502				
2775	Lynch, Alice			1058	Dermot O'Connor			1
2733	Lynch, Alice 'Alicia'	c.1809	Apr 1852/40y	2724	Patrick Henry Lynch	Dec 1838	2	1
1884	Lynch, Alice Blosse		1919	1875				
1895	Lynch, Alice Victoria		1939	1876	George G Soote			1
2271	Lynch, Ambrose						1	1
1621	Lynch, Ana 'y Ortiz'	1861	1947	1619	Roberto '. Guevara	1884	1	1
1260	Lynch, Anastacia			699	William Kirwan			1
1777	Lynch, Anastacia			1275				
2275	Lynch, Anastacia '.			2270				
2835	Lynch, Anastacia '.			2830	John Farrell			1
570	Lynch, Anastacia '.			564				
2596	Lynch, Anastacia '.	c.1742		2573				
1486	Lynch, Andrew			1296	Anne Joyce		4	1
1725	Lynch, Andrew	c 1620		1714				
2280	Lynch, Andrew						1	1
2284	Lynch, Andrew			2267				
2413	Lynch, Andrew		3 May 1664	2864			2	1
2605	Lynch, Andrew						1	1
2608	Lynch, Andrew			2606	??? Deane	1614	1	1
2612	Lynch, Andrew			2610	??? Lynch	1672	1	1
2616	Lynch, Andrew			2614	Margaret Mahon	1741	5	1
2623	Lynch, Andrew			2620				
2684	Lynch, Andrew			2681				
2699	Lynch, Andrew			2691	Elizabeth Cullen			1
665	Lynch, Andrew			579				
2382	Lynch, Andrew (Bishop)		1673	2380				
2106	Lynch, Andrew						1	1
1289	Lynch, Andrew (Mayor?)		25 Mar 1523	1262	Eleanor Martin		3	1
2678	Lynch, Andrew Henry		14 Jul 1847	2673	Theresa Butler			1
2156	Lynch, Annabel			2157	Valentine (1st Blake			1
2914	Lynch, Annabel '.			2915	George Dolphin	bef 1766		1
1070	Lynch, Annabel '.			1068				
1330	Lynch, Anne	1684		1315	John Lynch	8 Sep 1706		1
1400	Lynch, Anne			1395				
1420	Lynch, Anne			1407				1
1694	Lynch, Anne			1695	George Staunton	1701	1	1
2416	Lynch, Anne		22 Nov 1744	2415	Marcus 'Mark' Lynch	16 Jun 1707	2	1
2518	Lynch, Anne			2510				
2895	Lynch, Anne			825				
2958	Lynch, Anne			2592	Christopher Devenish			1
2996	Lynch, Anne			2989				

Num	Name	Birth date	Died	Father	Spouse	Married	Ch	M
599	Lynch, Anne			582	Garrett Warren			1
649	Lynch, Anne			647	Maurice Blake	1815	2	1
783	Lynch, Anne			775				
804	Lynch, Anne			858	Philip Higgins			1
826	Lynch, Anne	c.1743		810	Henry Browne			1
1596	Lynch, Anne 'Anna B.			1506				
1931	Lynch, Anne 'Anna V.			1927	? (Major) Foster			1
2840	Lynch, Anne 'Nancy'			2830				
1369	Lynch, Anthony			1352	Celia Burke	27 Jul 1801	6	1
1407	Lynch, Anthony		24 Mar 1903	1392	Henrietta Darcy	10 Feb 1872	6	1
1416	Lynch, Anthony			1407	Margaret Lillias	23 Apr 1903		1
2285	Lynch, Anthony			2267				
2966	Lynch, Anthony			2829				
588	Lynch, Anthony			582				
653	Lynch, Anthony			579			1	1
1591	Lynch, Anthony '.			1506			2	1
2267	Lynch, Anthony		Nov 1638	2270	Joan '. French		13	1
1394	Lynch, Anthony (Friar)			1369				
1332	Lynch, Anthony fitz						1	1
2732	Lynch, Arthur	c.1819		2724				
2768	Lynch, Arthur			2581				
2903	Lynch, Arthur		24 Jun 1892	638				
2915	Lynch, Arthur						1	1
2970	Lynch, Arthur		c.1751		Mary French			1
672	Lynch, Arthur		c 1530	674	Janetta ZZ?		1	1
863	Lynch, Arthur		1691	729	Joan Browne		1	1
1293	Lynch, Arthur (Mayor)		1539	1289				
2578	Lynch, Arthur Henry			2576	Frances Blake	18 Nov 1812	5	1
1600	Lynch, Arthur Jacques			1591				
2858	Lynch, Arthur Noel H.	c.1823	1879	1869				
1548	Lynch, Barbara			1540	Dominick Burke			1
1907	Lynch, Barbara		1904	1684	??? (Lt Geoghegan	1851		1
2702	Lynch, Barbara	c.1803		2593	Peter Harvey Lynch		1	1
3050	Lynch, Barbara			765				
842	Lynch, Barbara	c.1783		830				
2514	Lynch, Bartholomew '.			2510				
2646	Lynch, Beatrice			2642	Arthur Purser		3	1
216	Lynch, Benin	c 1957		126	Nora Byrne		1	1
1632	Lynch, Benito			1630				
1630	Lynch, Benito 'y A.			1628			1	1
1626	Lynch, Benito 'y Roo'			1615				
1432	Lynch, Bridget			1425	Oliver Nugent			1
2800	Lynch, Bridget				Martin Richardson			1
798	Lynch, Bridget			858	Anthony '. Madden			1
841	Lynch, Bridget	c.1780		830				
2547	Lynch, Bridget 'Delia'	c.1909		1443				
3069	Lynch, Brownlow (Rev)	1816		1869				
1885	Lynch, Caroline Blosse		1917	1875				
3023	Lynch, Caroline Mgt J	24 Jan 1960		3020				
1389	Lynch, Catherine			1352				
1399	Lynch, Catherine			1369				
1663	Lynch, Catherine			1643	Robert Skerrett	1 Jun 1712	1	1
2086	Lynch, Catherine			2079				
2725	Lynch, Catherine			2592	Francis (Capt) Eager			1
2740	Lynch, Catherine	c.1814		2724	Myles McDonnell			1
2763	Lynch, Catherine			2578				
2885	Lynch, Catherine			830				
2938	Lynch, Catherine			2937	James Hanly			1
2952	Lynch, Catherine			2593	??? de Vere Hunt			1
2995	Lynch, Catherine			2989				
571	Lynch, Catherine			564				
633	Lynch, Catherine			626				
802	Lynch, Catherine			858	??? Moore			1

An extract from the database of 2843 individuals (1 October 2013) including the Anglo-Norman Lynches who settled in Galway and members of my extended family (PaulBMcNulty.com on http://www.myfamily) (Ch = number of children; M = number of marriages).

Num	Name	Birth date	Died	Father	Spouse	Married	Ch	M
814	Lynch, Catherine			765	Theobold Burke			1
1553	Lynch, Catherine '.		17 Jan 1711	1554	Ulick Burke		2	1
2545	Lynch, Catherine '.	c.1904		1443	Timothy 'Tim' Walsh			1
2103	Lynch, Catherine (Sr)			1868				
926	Lynch, Catherine ?			927	John Darcy	1752?	1	1
2491	Lynch, Catherine M V.	1873		644				
1401	Lynch, Cecilia			1395				
1413	Lynch, Cecilia	c.1840		1392	John (BL) Fallon	19 Jul 1865		1
840	Lynch, Cecilia	c.1775		830				
590	Lynch, Cecilia '.			582	Patrick '. Lynch			1
774	Lynch, Cecilia 'Celia'			1533	Henry Lynch		4	1
2576	Lynch, Charles		c.1798	1567	Margaret French		5	1
2581	Lynch, Charles	1814	1863	2578	Charlotte Livesay		2	1
2599	Lynch, Charles	c.1810	Mar 1897	2724	Helena Joyce		2	1
2625	Lynch, Charles		1819	2620	Thomasina McMahon	1809		1
2957	Lynch, Charles			2599				
1933	Lynch, Charles French		23 Dec 1882	1547				
2809	Lynch, Charles John				Anne McMullen	c.1821		1
1268	Lynch, Christina			1285	John Mares		1	1
582	Lynch, Christopher		15 Dec 1635	579	Mary Lynch		13	1
2561	Lynch, Claire			216				
3025	Lynch, Clare Annabel	16 Feb 1969		3020				
636	Lynch, Clarinda			626				
1893	Lynch, Constance Emily		1943	1876	C (Dr) O'Rourke			1
1479	Lynch, David 'de'			1481			1	1
2666	Lynch, Denis			2644				
1313	Lynch, Dominick			1303				
1533	Lynch, Dominick			1540			4	1
1714	Lynch, Dominick	c 1597	1638	1300	Mary ? French		5	1
2293	Lynch, Dominick				Mary Lynch			1
2462	Lynch, Dominick			2461				
2904	Lynch, Dominick	c.1681	c.Jul 1764/83y				1	1
862	Lynch, Dominick		bef 1713 osp	744				
1275	Lynch, Dominick 'Duff'		1508	1281	Anastacia Martin		7	2
1651	Lynch, Dominick (Dr)	1697	1639					
1294	Lynch, Dominick		28 Mar 1594	1291	Eleanor (Dame) Lynch		7	1
883	Lynch, Dominick ?			693			1	1
2841	Lynch, Edmond			2831				
2907	Lynch, Edmond		8 Nov 1772/84y					
2861	Lynch, Edmond '.						1	1
890	Lynch, Edmund 'en T.		1462	695	Mary ZZ?		1	1
1381	Lynch, Edward			1352				
1391	Lynch, Edward			1369				
1430	Lynch, Edward			1425				
2665	Lynch, Edward			2644				
2899	Lynch, Edward			843				
1560	Lynch, Edward (Sir)		1783	1533				
1876	Lynch, Edward Patk (Lt	c.1809	23 May 1884	1869	Emily E. Stirton		6	1
2642	Lynch, Edward Whitby			2604	Lily Curtis		2	1
1350	Lynch, Eleanor	17 Oct 1711		1322	Pierce Blake	20 Feb 1737		1
1710	Lynch, Eleanor				George Staunton		1	1
2863	Lynch, Eleanor '.		c.1708	729	C. O'Shaughnessy		1	1
2967	Lynch, Eleanor '.			2829	Anthony Deaves			1
2110	Lynch, Eleanor '.				Thomas (4th Blake			1
740	Lynch, Eleanor '.	bef 1619	1692	581	Valentine (3rd Blake	27 Jun 1632	2	1
1295	Lynch, Eleanor (Dame)			1455	Dominick Lynch		7	1
1718	Lynch, Elizabeth			1714				
1890	Lynch, Elizabeth			1876	E S (Col) Marryott			1
2195	Lynch, Elizabeth	c 1735	20 Sep 1808		John (Rev) Vesey		2	2
2276	Lynch, Elizabeth			2270				
2695	Lynch, Elizabeth			2691	Thomas Cullen			1
2860	Lynch, Elizabeth		14 Sep 1626	2861				
736	Lynch, Elizabeth			581	Thomas ? Lynch		3	1

An extract from the database of 2843 individuals (1 October 2013) including the Anglo-Norman Lynches who settled in Galway and members of my extended family (PaulBMcNulty.com on http://www.myfamily) (Ch = number of children; M = number of marriages).

Num	Name	Birth date	Died	Father	Spouse	Married	Ch	M
757	Lynch, Elizabeth			729				
781	Lynch, Elizabeth			775	Andrew Crean-Lynch	Jan 1811		1
1911	Lynch, Elizabeth '.		1906	1684				
2950	Lynch, Elizabeth '.			2593	??? ? McDonald			1
806	Lynch, Elizabeth '.			858	??? Merrick			1
956	Lynch, Elizabeth '.			810	Geoffrey '. Browne			1
598	Lynch, Elizabeth '.			582				
1741	Lynch, Elizabeth '.		bef 1642	1764	Roger O'Shaughnessy		2	1
2777	Lynch, Elizabeth ?			2772	John Darcy	c.1752		1
1580	Lynch, Elizabeth Marie			1505				
1909	Lynch, Ellen		1892	1684	Edward T. Stapleton	1855		1
2746	Lynch, Ellen			1563	??? Darcy		1	1
694	Lynch, Ellen			909	James Lynch		4	1
1904	Lynch, Ellen (Sr) W.	6 Oct 1867	25 Feb 1905	1681				
3047	Lynch, Ellis			765	John French			2
2668	Lynch, Emily			2644				
3024	Lynch, Emily Jane B.	16 Sep 1967		3020				
1627	Lynch, Estanislao 'y			1615	Carmen de y Zaldivar		1	1
2490	Lynch, Ethcl	1871		644				
592	Lynch, Evelyn			582				
602	Lynch, Evelyn			582				
2161	Lynch, Evelyn '.			2393	Valentine Blake		1	1
2507	Lynch, Evelyn '.			2508	Stephen Browne		1	1
2792	Lynch, Eyre		c.1851	2829				
2764	Lynch, Frances			2578	Joseph S Blake			1
635	Lynch, Frances			626				
1913	Lynch, Frances 'Fanny'			1684				
1905	Lynch, Frances (Sr)	4 Feb 1869	19 Oct 1956	1681				
1395	Lynch, Francis			1369	Harriet Blake		4	1
1411	Lynch, Francis			1392				
1868	Lynch, Francis		c.1804	2070	Julia Blake		7	1
2075	Lynch, Francis			2073				
2098	Lynch, Francis			1868				
214	Lynch, Francis	c 1956		126				
2522	Lynch, Francis	c. 1824		2076				
2664	Lynch, Francis		c.1916	2644				1
2831	Lynch, Francis						2	1
2890	Lynch, Francis			825				
2940	Lynch, Francis			2707				
2812	Lynch, Francis Joseph			2813				
1619	Lynch, Francisco 'y	1817		1617	Eloisa Ortiz	1854	1	1
2855	Lynch, Frederick B.	c.1822	5 Nov 1834	1869				
1775	Lynch, Gabriel			1275				
3053	Lynch, Garrett	c.1727		810				
2294	Lynch, Garrett '.			2267	Dominick Darcy			1
1493	Lynch, Geoffrey			1296				
1724	Lynch, Geoffrey	c 1617		1714				
2393	Lynch, Geoffrey						1	1
2508	Lynch, Geoffrey						1	1
1300	Lynch, Geoffrey (MP)		1627-32	1294	Elizabeth Browne		5	1
699	Lynch, Geoffrey Walter			890	??? Font		2	1
2710	Lynch, George		1875	2707			2	1
838	Lynch, George	c.1783		830				
2856	Lynch, George Quested	c.1813	26 Jul 1848/35	1869				
129	Lynch, Gerard	c 1953		126				
127	Lynch, Gerarda	c 1950		126	Anthony '. McHugh		2	1
1594	Lynch, Guillemette F.			1506	Ralph Clavering		1	1
2601	Lynch, H??				??? French		1	1
1404	Lynch, Harriet			1395	John H Blake			1
2754	Lynch, Harriet			2576	??? Hopkins			1
2810	Lynch, Harriet '.			2811				
856	Lynch, Harriet '.		8 Aug 1755	810	Dominick Browne	18 Nov 1754	1	1
2489	Lynch, Harriet E M B	1869		644				

An extract from the database of 2843 individuals (1 October 2013) including the Anglo-Norman Lynches who settled in Galway and members of my extended family (PaulBMcNulty.com on http://www.myfamily) (Ch = number of children; M = number of marriages).

Num	Name	Birth date	Died	Father	Spouse	Married	Ch	M
2640	Lynch, Helen			2604				
2651	Lynch, Helen			2642	Harry Filmer			1
2520	Lynch, Henrietta			2510				
637	Lynch, Henrietta			626				
1302	Lynch, Henry			1294				
1464	Lynch, Henry			1460	Helen O'Shaughnessy		1	1
1476	Lynch, Henry						1	1
1494	Lynch, Henry			1296				
2281	Lynch, Henry			2267				
2513	Lynch, Henry			2510				
2592	Lynch, Henry	c.1744	1820	2573	Margaret Browne		4	2
2606	Lynch, Henry			2605	??? Bodkin	1579	1	1
2610	Lynch, Henry			2608	??? French	1644	1	1
2614	Lynch, Henry			2612	Mary Kirwan	1703	1	1
2620	Lynch, Henry	1753	14 Dec 1814	2616	Catherine Hevey		5	1
2634	Lynch, Henry	1824	1870	2629	Jane Joyce	1860	1	1
2717	Lynch, Henry			2594	Alicia Browne	8 Dec 1840		1
2730	Lynch, Henry	c.1808		2724				
2891	Lynch, Henry			825				
2898	Lynch, Henry			843				
2910	Lynch, Henry		bef 1752				1	1
3042	Lynch, Henry			581				
676	Lynch, Henry			678			1	1
773	Lynch, Henry		c.1777-1780	858	Cecilia '. Lynch		4	2
887	Lynch, Henry			695			1	1
787	Lynch, Henry 'of C.		1819	773				
581	Lynch, Henry (1st Bt)		21 Feb 1634	579	Elizabeth Martin		9	1
744	Lynch, Henry (3rd Bt)	bef 1634	28 Aug 1691	729	Margaret '. Burke		5	2
810	Lynch, Henry (5th Bt)	29 Sep 1699	28 Jul 1762/62	765	Mary Moore	1722	6	1
1875	Lynch, Henry (Capt)	24 Nov 1807	1872	1869	Caroline Taylor	Aug 1838	4	1
1887	Lynch, Henry (Col) B.	16 Dec 1856	7 Jan 1936	1876	Emily G. Graham	16 Jun 1898	1	1
1869	Lynch, Henry (Major)	1778	1 Jun 1823	1863	Elizabeth Finnis	1800	11	1
3020	Lynch, Henry (Major)	17 Jun 1933		3017	Janet Duveen Horsley	14 Oct 1966	4	1
2644	Lynch, Henry Charles			2604	Alice Vaughan		8	1
3022	Lynch, Henry Charles	25 Aug 1972		3020				
777	Lynch, Henry Edward	c.1780		775				
2600	Lynch, Henry Ffrench	c.1856	c.Jul 1921/65y	2601	??? Hackett			1
2735	Lynch, Henry Michael			2734	??? Regan			1
3017	Lynch, Henry Pk (Col)	30 Apr 1899		1887	Lois Burnley Yate	11 Apr 1931	2	1
2969	Lynch, Honor			2829				
2713	Lynch, Ignatius		c.1721	1563	Mary Morris		1	1
2852	Lynch, Ignatius			729				
2458	Lynch, Isabella 'Bell'			2459	Hyacinth Bodkin		1	1
1058	Lynch, Isidore	bef 1635	1697	1296			3	1
1474	Lynch, Isidore			1470	Mary Lynch		1	2
2758	Lynch, Isidore			2578	Celia Blake		1	2
927	Lynch, Isidore (Col)			2827	Sybil Blake		2	1
1478	Lynch, Isidore (Lt G.	7 Jun 1755	4 Aug 1841	1474				
1068	Lynch, James				Margaret '. Blake		2	1
1485	Lynch, James			1289				
1499	Lynch, James			1486				
2107	Lynch, James						1	1
2157	Lynch, James						1	1
2273	Lynch, James			2272				
2376	Lynch, James			1764			1	1
2418	Lynch, James		c.1765				1	1
2681	Lynch, James		1847	2616	??? Kelly		3	1
2786	Lynch, James	c.1749	1765	2417				
2888	Lynch, James			825				
2964	Lynch, James			2829				
2972	Lynch, James		c.1750	2973				
693	Lynch, James		c.1400	691	Ellen Lynch		4	2
701	Lynch, James			699	Agnes Lynch		1	1

An extract from the database of 2843 individuals (1 October 2013) including the Anglo-Norman Lynches who settled in Galway and members of my extended family (PaulBMcNulty.com on http://www.myfamily) (Ch = number of children; M = number of marriages).

Num	Name	Birth date	Died	Father	Spouse	Married	Ch	M
769	Lynch, James			744				
2270	Lynch, James			2271			6	1
3037	Lynch, James		1713					
1286	Lynch, James (Mayor)			1262	??? Blake		2	1
684	Lynch, James Walter?			686			1	1
1708	Lynch, Jane			1611				
2517	Lynch, Jane			2510				
2618	Lynch, Jane		23 Aug 1819	2616	James Rooney			1
2896	Lynch, Jane			825				
634	Lynch, Jane			626				
795	Lynch, Jane			773	Isidore Blake			1
816	Lynch, Jane		c.1760	765	John Darcy		2	1
953	Lynch, Jane			620	Laurence Comyn	24 Mar 1800		1
1585	Lynch, Jane Jeanne C.			1502	Michel David Kirwan			1
1349	Lynch, Janet	21 Oct 1705		1322				
1719	Lynch, Janet 'Gennet'			1294				
3041	Lynch, Janet 'Jennet'			581				
1936	Lynch, Janet Jeanette			1547	Abraham F Royse	c.1830		1
2628	Lynch, Jasper			2620				
2574	Lynch, Joan			1565	Arthur French		2	1
2597	Lynch, Joan			2573				
574	Lynch, Joan 'Joane'			564				
1256	Lynch, Joan 'Joanna'			887	Richard Bodkin			1
1283	Lynch, Joan 'Joanna'			1273	John 'O' Fallon			1
1367	Lynch, Joan 'Joanna'		1822	1337	Michael Burke	1766		1
1384	Lynch, Joan 'Joanna'			1352	Patrick Farrell			1
603	Lynch, Joan 'Juan'?			582				
1281	Lynch, John			883			3	1
1297	Lynch, John			1294				
1303	Lynch, John	c.1612	3 Sep 1691	1300	Mary Lynch	30 Jul 1641	4	1
1331	Lynch, John			1332	Anne Lynch	8 Sep 1706		1
1335	Lynch, John	10 Apr 1713		1322				
1423	Lynch, John			895	C. Bermingham		1	1
1436	Lynch, John		c 1808	1425				
1490	Lynch, John			1296				
1773	Lynch, John			1275				
2078	Lynch, John			2073				
2286	Lynch, John			2267				
2414	Lynch, John		14 Feb 1678	2413				
2459	Lynch, John						1	1
2516	Lynch, John			2510				
2593	Lynch, John			2573	Barbara Cuniss		8	2
2624	Lynch, John			2620				
2685	Lynch, John			2681				
2706	Lynch, John		1884	2593				
2709	Lynch, John			2707				
2832	Lynch, John			2830				
2887	Lynch, John			825				
2945	Lynch, John			2944				
586	Lynch, John			582				
655	Lynch, John			653				
663	Lynch, John			659				
680	Lynch, John			682			1	1
837	Lynch, John	c.1777		830				
858	Lynch, John			765	Mary 'Brown' Browne		7	1
911	Lynch, John						1	1
2104	Lynch, John 'de'			2106			1	1
1575	Lynch, John 'Jean B.	3 Jun 1749	16 Aug 1835	1505	Marie C. Le Berthon		1	2
1502	Lynch, John 'Jean'	1669		1495	Guillemette Constant	26 Nov 1709	4	1
1589	Lynch, John 'Jean'	c 1746	1756/10y	1506				
1506	Lynch, John 'Jean' A.		1774	1502	Mary 'Marie' French		9	2
1588	Lynch, John 'Jean' M.	31 Mar 1744	c.1825	1506				
584	Lynch, John (Bishop)	1533	1603	2107			1	1

An extract from the database of 2843 individuals (1 October 2013) including the Anglo-Norman Lynches who settled in Galway and members of my extended family (PaulBMcNulty.com on http://www.myfamily) (Ch = number of children; M = number of marriages).

Num	Name	Birth date	Died	Father	Spouse	Married	Ch	M
1291	Lynch, John (Mayor)		1572	1289	Redish (Dame) Lynch		1	1
2441	Lynch, John (Rev)			2439				
1782	Lynch, John Alexander	c 1756		1781				
2543	Lynch, John Arthur B	1874	1892/18y	644				
780	Lynch, John Bermingham			775				
2989	Lynch, John Brown		c.1845	2087	Mary Morgan		6	1
1873	Lynch, John Finnis	7 Apr 1805	7 Oct 1855	1869				
1784	Lynch, John Mareschall				Agnes 'de' Vale			1
2643	Lynch, John Patrick	7 Dec 1858	1920	2604	Frieda Ottman	7 Dec 1896	3	1
1681	Lynch, John Wilson	1831	c.1911-29	1684	Frances Redington	5 Jul 1865	5	1
1378	Lynch, Jonathan				Catherine Burke			1
2691	Lynch, Jonathan		15 Sep 1841	2616	Catherine Hynes		4	1
1563	Lynch, Joseph			734	Margaret Blake	1675	4	1
1569	Lynch, Joseph		c.1787	1567			1	1
1658	Lynch, Joseph			1652	??? 'Joyes' Joyce		1	1
1660	Lynch, Joseph			1658				
1855	Lynch, Joseph		1721	863	Anstace Blake	1712	1	1
1863	Lynch, Joseph	c.1744	1785	1861	Margaret Maria Blake	1766	2	1
2510	Lynch, Joseph		c.1813		Margaret Blake		8	1
2714	Lynch, Joseph			2713	Jane ZZ?			1
2753	Lynch, Joseph		1837	2576				
2862	Lynch, Joseph		1 Jun 1863/49y					
760	Lynch, Judith			729	Robert Martin			1
1382	Lynch, Julia			1352	Walter Martin	1800		1
2085	Lynch, Julia			2079				
2094	Lynch, Julia			2087				
2443	Lynch, Julia			2439	Arthur French			1
2494	Lynch, Julia		c.1686		Oliver (Capt) Browne	c.1655	1	1
2728	Lynch, Julia	c.1791		2576	Peter (Capt) Lynch	1809?	8	1
2751	Lynch, Julia			1567	Francis French	2 Sep 1771		1
2837	Lynch, Julia			2830	??? Bodkin			1
2997	Lynch, Julia			2989				
618	Lynch, Julia			614	Hyacinth Darcy	1784	2	1
1717	Lynch, Julia 'Julian'	c 1603		1300				
1727	Lynch, Julia 'Julian'	c 1623		1714				
2274	Lynch, Julia 'Julian'			2270				
2894	Lynch, Julia 'Julian'			825				
573	Lynch, Julia 'Julian'			564				
762	Lynch, Julia 'Julian'			729	Walter Blake			1
2419	Lynch, Julia 'Juliane'		c.1790	2417	George Blake	18 Apr 1728	3	1
2096	Lynch, Julia 'Julie'			1868	Dominick Crean-Lynch			1
1615	Lynch, Justo P 'y G.	1755		1613	Ana B y Cabezas Roo	1786	3	1
1274	Lynch, Kathleen			1275	Oliver Lynch		1	1
1705	Lynch, Kathleen			1611				
1419	Lynch, Kathleen (Sr)			1407				
2587	Lynch, Kathleen Mary			2584	Denis (Capt) Daly	3 Jun 1899	2	1
130	Lynch, Kevin	c 1954		126				
587	Lynch, Lazarus			582				
1892	Lynch, Louisa Caroline							
1897	Lynch, Louisa Caroline		1913	1876				
1934	Lynch, Lucy			1547	Richard Martin			1
2519	Lynch, Lucy Ann			2510				
2857	Lynch, Lucy Anne B.			1863				
2823	Lynch, Mabella			2822				
2016	Lynch, Magdalene '.			2017	Dominick Joyce		2	1
128	Lynch, Majella	c 1951		126				
2641	Lynch, Marcella			2604				
1046	Lynch, Marcus		bef 1677	1437			1	1
1059	Lynch, Marcus	bef 1635		1296				
2017	Lynch, Marcus						1	1
2415	Lynch, Marcus		14 Jul 1725	2413	Mary French	28 Jul 1679	1	1
2778	Lynch, Marcus			2772			1	1
2833	Lynch, Marcus			2830				

An extract from the database of 2843 individuals (1 October 2013) including the Anglo-Norman Lynches who settled in Galway and members of my extended family (PaulBMcNulty.com on http://www.myfamily) (Ch = number of children; M = number of marriages).

Num	Name	Birth date	Died	Father	Spouse	Married	Ch	M
604	Lynch, Marcus			608	Elizabeth Browne	1684	1	1
614	Lynch, Marcus		1787	610	Anstace Blake	1742	3	2
647	Lynch, Marcus		1816	614	Mary Blake	24 Jan 1794	1	1
705	Lynch, Marcus			701	Catherine Neale		1	1
1547	Lynch, Marcus 'Mark'	1755	1822	1941	Barbara Burke	Mar 1785	8	2
1947	Lynch, Marcus 'Mark'	1684			Jane Biggs		2	1
2087	Lynch, Marcus 'Mark'			1868	??? Browne		4	1
2380	Lynch, Marcus 'Mark'			2379	Mary Lynch		1	1
2417	Lynch, Marcus 'Mark'		23 Sep 1749	2418	Anne Lynch	16 Jun 1707	3	2
2965	Lynch, Marcus 'Mark'			2829				
1952	Lynch, Marcus 'Mark' ?			1684				
1898	Lynch, Marcus (Dr) W.	1866/26y	1892	1681				
1439	Lynch, Marcus (Mayor)		c.1610	1441			1	1
626	Lynch, Marcus Blake		Jan 1829	620	Jane-Mary Byrne	Jan 1792	6	2
2986	Lynch, Marcus Duff			670				
1901	Lynch, Marcus F Wilson	1903		1682				
644	Lynch, Marcus Nicholas	12 Sep 1836	6 Nov 1916	638	Blanche de Marylski	1867	5	1
1386	Lynch, Margaret			1352	John Doherty			1
1571	Lynch, Margaret			1569	Christopher Dillon	10 Feb 1794		1
1661	Lynch, Margaret	c 1697		1652	Thomas Redington	1719 or 172	1	1
1706	Lynch, Margaret			1611				
1772	Lynch, Margaret			1281				
1779	Lynch, Margaret			1277				
1940	Lynch, Margaret			1547				
2004	Lynch, Margaret			2009	Edmond Athy		7	1
2020	Lynch, Margaret			2021	Edmond Athy		1	1
2277	Lynch, Margaret			2270				
2546	Lynch, Margaret	c.1906		1443				
2677	Lynch, Margaret			2673				
2697	Lynch, Margaret		20 Mar 1820	2691	Henry T. Redmond			1
2727	Lynch, Margaret		bef 1820	2592				
2738	Lynch, Margaret	c.1811		2724	Thomas Fair			1
2942	Lynch, Margaret			2710				
2946	Lynch, Margaret			2703	Edward (QC) Beytagh		2	1
601	Lynch, Margaret			582				
645	Lynch, Margaret	c 1838	27 Apr 1930	638				
864	Lynch, Margaret			729				
2549	Lynch, Margaret '.	c.1877		1450				
1264	Lynch, Margaret '.			1262				
1577	Lynch, Margaret '.			1575				
1583	Lynch, Margaret '.			1505				
1322	Lynch, Martin			1315	Joan French	19 Apr 1702	6	1
1352	Lynch, Martin	30 May 1745		1337	Margaret Burke		8	1
1379	Lynch, Martin	c.1780		1352	Miss St George			1
1390	Lynch, Martin			1369				
1406	Lynch, Martin			1392				
2076	Lynch, Martin			2073			2	1
2278	Lynch, Martin			2267	Mary Lynch			1
2780	Lynch, Martin			2779				
2892	Lynch, Martin			825				
2922	Lynch, Martin		bef 1766		Deborah ZZ?			1
662	Lynch, Martin			659				
2865	Lynch, Martin (BL) B.	3 Oct 1731	c.1799	2420	Julia '. Kirwan			1
2797	Lynch, Martin (BL) F.				Jane Eyre			1
2509	Lynch, Martin ?			927				
1304	Lynch, Mary		18 Dec 1677	1305	John Lynch	30 Jul 1641	4	1
1326	Lynch, Mary	10 Dec 1672	c.1741	1315	Oliver 'Joyes' Joyce	c.1695		1
1388	Lynch, Mary			1352				
1402	Lynch, Mary		1909	1395	C? T Boothman			1
1475	Lynch, Mary			1476	Isidore Lynch		1	1
1513	Lynch, Mary			775				
1532	Lynch, Mary			1533	Andrew Crean	6 Jan 1751	4	1
1542	Lynch, Mary			1540	Myles Burke	1718	1	1

Num	Name	Birth date	Died	Father	Spouse	Married	Ch	M
1642	Lynch, Mary				Thomas Skerrett		1	1
1716	Lynch, Mary	c 1600		1300				
2084	Lynch, Mary			2079				
2091	Lynch, Mary			2087				
2108	Lynch, Mary			1781	John Bushell			1
2279	Lynch, Mary			2280	Martin Lynch			1
2292	Lynch, Mary			2267	Dominick Lynch			1
2296	Lynch, Mary			2267	Valentine French			1
2381	Lynch, Mary				Marcus 'Mark' Lynch		1	1
2424	Lynch, Mary			2417	Thomas Browne			1
2598	Lynch, Mary			2573				
2667	Lynch, Mary			2644				
2675	Lynch, Mary		1872	2673	James Joyce		1	1
2686	Lynch, Mary			2681	Patrick Joyce		2	1
2693	Lynch, Mary			2691	James Stanley			1
2766	Lynch, Mary			2578	Arthur Crean			1
2773	Lynch, Mary			1058	John Blake			1
2802	Lynch, Mary				Luke Dodgworth	4 Jul 1807		1
2893	Lynch, Mary			825				
2993	Lynch, Mary			2989	??? Golding			1
572	Lynch, Mary			564				
583	Lynch, Mary			584	Christopher Lynch		13	1
595	Lynch, Mary			582	Edward Byellagh?		2	1
611	Lynch, Mary			612	Nicholas Lynch		1	1
722	Lynch, Mary			713	Robert (Sir) Jacob		5	1
738	Lynch, Mary		29 Jul 1671	581	Geoffrey '. Browne		2	1
755	Lynch, Mary			751	Thomas Blake			1
759	Lynch, Mary			729	Thomas Nolan			1
800	Lynch, Mary			858	Joseph McDonnell			1
894	Lynch, Mary			744	Stephen Lynch		1	1
2943	Lynch, Mary 'Mamie'			2710				
2485	Lynch, Mary 'Maria'			3033	John Ormsby		1	1
2495	Lynch, Mary 'Maria'		1627		Martin Browne		1	1
2799	Lynch, Mary 'Maria'				Joseph Kirwan	24 Nov 1800		1
2445	Lynch, Mary 'Marie'		1730	2439	Oliver Bodkin	c. 1720	1	1
2402	Lynch, Mary 'Marie'				Ulick (1st E. Burke		1	2
1601	Lynch, Mary 'Marie' D			1591				
1581	Lynch, Mary 'Marie' M			1505				
1584	Lynch, Mary 'Marie'			1505				
1579	Lynch, Mary 'Marie'			1505				
2905	Lynch, Mary 'Molly'			2904	John Kelly	c.1751		1
2897	Lynch, Mary Ann	c.1805		825				
839	Lynch, Mary Anne	c.1775		830				
2935	Lynch, Mary Browne or				Peter Skerrett			1
1912	Lynch, Mary Jane			1684				
2941	Lynch, Matilda			2707				
1308	Lynch, Matthew '.			1305				
2440	Lynch, Matthew (Capt)			2439				
1946	Lynch, Matthew Martin?			1941				
2544	Lynch, Maud	c.1903		1443	??? O'Grady			1
2657	Lynch, Maureen			2643				
1902	Lynch, Maureen Wilson	2 Mar 1906	May 2000	1682	James John Smyth	8 Jun 1935		1
1565	Lynch, Maurice		1747	1563	??? Darcy	c.1701	2	1
2079	Lynch, Maurice			1868	Julia ? Browne		4	1
734	Lynch, Maurice '.		c.1683	581	Joan 'Jennet' French	c.1632	1	1
1450	Lynch, Michael	c.1809	1899/90y	2539	Mary ZZ?	c.1870/73	3	1
1607	Lynch, Michael				Mary Browne		1	1
1861	Lynch, Michael		1771	1855	Anastacia '. Blake	1740	1	1
2283	Lynch, Michael			2267				
2442	Lynch, Michael			2439				
2515	Lynch, Michael			2510				
2816	Lynch, Michael			2817	Anne Lewen	27 Oct 1851		1
3056	Lynch, Michael			751				

An extract from the database of 2843 individuals (1 October 2013) including the Anglo-Norman Lynches who settled in Galway and members of my extended family (PaulBMcNulty.com on http://www.myfamily) (Ch = number of children; M = number of marriages).

Num	Name	Birth date	Died	Father	Spouse	Married	Ch	M
1652	Lynch, Michael (Capt)	c 1670	1750/80y	1643	Elizabeth Darcy		2	1
2540	Lynch, Michael ?						1	1
2562	Lynch, Michael ?			1450				
836	Lynch, Michael Henry	c.1774		830				
2991	Lynch, Michael John			2989				
2909	Lynch, Monica			2910	Michael Bonfield	7 Feb 1752		1
1595	Lynch, Monique	1754		1506	Patrick French	1774		1
2829	Lynch, Neptune		c.1794		Honoria ZZ?		6	1
612	Lynch, Neptune						1	1
1298	Lynch, Nicholas			1294				
1336	Lynch, Nicholas			1322				
1491	Lynch, Nicholas			1296				
1695	Lynch, Nicholas						1	1
1726	Lynch, Nicholas	c 1622		1714				
1951	Lynch, Nicholas		dsp	1947				
2487	Lynch, Nicholas			608			1	1
2811	Lynch, Nicholas						1	1
2813	Lynch, Nicholas						1	1
2814	Lynch, Nicholas			2815				
2815	Lynch, Nicholas						1	1
2830	Lynch, Nicholas		c.1740	2831			7	1
2853	Lynch, Nicholas			729				
3045	Lynch, Nicholas			744				
3051	Lynch, Nicholas			765				
568	Lynch, Nicholas			564				
608	Lynch, Nicholas		c 1688	1046	Catherine '. Browne		3	2
610	Lynch, Nicholas		c 1725	604	Mary Lynch		1	2
620	Lynch, Nicholas			614	Catherine Blake	1765	3	1
638	Lynch, Nicholas	22 Feb 1804	22 Nov 1862	626	Elizabeth '. Grehan	24 Nov 1835	3	1
664	Lynch, Nicholas			579				
717	Lynch, Nicholas			713	Elizabeth Lambert		1	1
733	Lynch, Nicholas			581				
888	Lynch, Nicholas			695				
1244	Lynch, Nicholas (Capt)		1900	644				
1441	Lynch, Nicholas		c 1567	1277			1	1
579	Lynch, Nicholas			670			8	1
909	Lynch, Nicholas duff			911			1	1
1437	Lynch, Nicholas More		c 1650	1439			1	1
2658	Lynch, Olga			2643				
1273	Lynch, Oliver		1511	1271	Kathleen Lynch		1	1
1307	Lynch, P?			1305				
1634	Lynch, Patricio		1886	1627				
1314	Lynch, Patrick			1303				
1443	Lynch, Patrick	c.1862		1450	Ellen Cooke	14 Aug 1902	6	1
1516	Lynch, Patrick						1	1
1611	Lynch, Patrick			1609	Agnes 'Ines' Blake		7	1
1941	Lynch, Patrick	1714		1947	Anne French	1747	2	1
213	Lynch, Patrick	c 1955		126				
2539	Lynch, Patrick	c.1791	28 Mar 1869	2540			1	1
2629	Lynch, Patrick	1790		2620	Marcella Flanagan	1820	2	2
2673	Lynch, Patrick		14 Jan 1830	2616	Jane Kelly		4	1
775	Lynch, Patrick		1813	773	Mary Blake	8 May 1780	6	2
591	Lynch, Patrick 'Linch'				Cecilia '. Lynch			1
1617	Lynch, Patrick 'P J y	1789	1881	1615	Maria y R. Zavaleta	1813	2	1
126	Lynch, Patrick 'Paddy'	11 Mar 1911	23 Feb 2009	1443	Bridget '. Higgins	15 Apr 1948	7	1
1592	Lynch, Patrick '.	5 Jul 1759		1506				
1590	Lynch, Patrick '.	26 Mar 1747	c 1751/4y	1506				
1613	Lynch, Patrick '.	1715		1611	Rosa de la Galayn	1749	1	1
2879	Lynch, Patrick (Dr)				Margaret Blake			1
2734	Lynch, Patrick Henry				Alice 'Alicia' Lynch	Dec 1838	2	1
2637	Lynch, Patrick Joseph	1861	aft 1914	2634				
1684	Lynch, Patrick Marcus	1785	1864	1547	Ellen Wilson	1820	8	1
778	Lynch, Patrick or P.			775	Anna Maria Fleeson			1

An extract from the database of 2843 individuals (1 October 2013) including the Anglo-Norman Lynches who settled in Galway and members of my extended family (PaulBMcNulty.com on http://www.myfamily) (Ch = number of children; M = number of marriages).

Num	Name	Birth date	Died	Father	Spouse	Married	Ch	M
1334	Lynch, Peter	26 Jul 1709		1322				
1501	Lynch, Peter			1486				
1637	Lynch, Peter				Mary Kirwan		1	1
1639	Lynch, Peter			1637	Mary Skerrett		2	1
1776	Lynch, Peter			1275				
2288	Lynch, Peter			2267				
2573	Lynch, Peter		1760	1563	Eliza Mgt? C. Field	c.1740	7	1
2595	Lynch, Peter			2573				
2707	Lynch, Peter		16 Sep 1852	2593	Julia Taaffe	1832	6	1
2711	Lynch, Peter			2707				
2745	Lynch, Peter			2599				
2886	Lynch, Peter	c.1790		825				
2955	Lynch, Peter			2593				
3043	Lynch, Peter			581				
751	Lynch, Peter			729	Bibyan O'Flaherty		2	1
825	Lynch, Peter	c.1728	1810	810			12	1
867	Lynch, Peter		1810	832				
1643	Lynch, Peter 'Pierce'			1639	Margaret Vigo		2	2
1574	Lynch, Peter 'Pierre'	15 Dec 1744	c 1748	1505				
1766	Lynch, Peter 'Pyerse'			1281	Eveline Blake	1468		1
2724	Lynch, Peter (Capt)	c.1781	1840	2592	Julia Lynch	1809?	8	1
1567	Lynch, Peter (Sir)		Dec 1772	1565	Mary Anne Mannion		4	1
2703	Lynch, Peter Harvey	c.1790		2576	Barbara Lynch		1	1
2737	Lynch, Peter Joseph			2734				
2005	Lynch, Philip		c.1716?	2009	Sarah Ormsby			1
2009	Lynch, Philip				Margaret Baynham		2	1
3033	Lynch, Philip						1	1
1882	Lynch, Quested Finnis	1841	26 Jul 1848	1875				
593	Lynch, Reddith			582	Andrew French			1
2676	Lynch, Reddith '.			2673				
2261	Lynch, Redish				John Lambert		1	1
1292	Lynch, Redish (Dame)			1516	John (Mayor) Lynch		1	1
1418	Lynch, Richard			1407				
1780	Lynch, Richard			1495			1	1
2662	Lynch, Richard			2644				
2807	Lynch, Richard				Judith Burke	8 Jul 1820		1
2584	Lynch, Richard Charles	c.1851		2581	Helena Mary Nugent	20 Jan 1876	1	1
1927	Lynch, Richard Marcus		12 Jun 1894	1547	Georgina Varenne		1	1
2083	Lynch, Robert			2079				
2731	Lynch, Robert	c.1816		2724				
674	Lynch, Robert			676			1	1
788	Lynch, Robert			773	Mary 'Brown' Browne			1
1455	Lynch, Robert 'Robuck'						1	1
729	Lynch, Robert 'Robuck'		c.1667	581	Ellis French	aft Apr 162	13	1
765	Lynch, Robert (4th Bt)			744	Catherine Blake	29 Nov 1683	7	1
818	Lynch, Robert (6th Bt)		1775	810	Elizabeth J. Barker	14 Jan 1749	2	1
2095	Lynch, Robert (Capt)		13 Mar 1861	1868	??? Irvine			1
1874	Lynch, Robert (Capt)	c.1806	21 May 1836	1869				
3036	Lynch, Roland (Bishop)							
2974	Lynch, Rose			2973				
1883	Lynch, Rose Blosse		1890	1875				
1422	Lynch, Rosina		1876	1407				
1888	Lynch, Sarah Jane	1844	1900	1876	Thomas A. Scott			1
3026	Lynch, Sheila G.	28 Feb 1932		3017	John Wilson-Wright	30 Jun 1953		1
882	Lynch, Sinolda de M.			688			1	1
2742	Lynch, Sophia			2724				
2661	Lynch, Stanislaus			2644				
2604	Lynch, Stanislaus J.	1831	1915	2629	Helen Briscoe		5	1
1069	Lynch, Stephen			1068				
1262	Lynch, Stephen			695	Joanna Penrise		4	2
1299	Lynch, Stephen			1294				
1425	Lynch, Stephen		25 Jun 1771	1423	Bridget ZZ?		4	2
1431	Lynch, Stephen		c 1787	1425				

An extract from the database of 2843 individuals (1 October 2013) including the Anglo-Norman Lynches who settled in Galway and members of my extended family (PaulBMcNulty.com on http://www.myfamily) (Ch = number of children; M = number of marriages).

Num	Name	Birth date	Died	Father	Spouse	Married	Ch	M
1492	Lynch, Stephen			1296				
1715	Lynch, Stephen	c 1606		1300				
2021	Lynch, Stephen						1	1
2272	Lynch, Stephen			2270			1	1
2663	Lynch, Stephen		aft 1928	2644				
2834	Lynch, Stephen			2830				
564	Lynch, Stephen		26 Nov 1636	579	Catherine Blake		7	1
646	Lynch, Stephen			608				
895	Lynch, Stephen	1660		1303	Mary Lynch		1	1
2476	Lynch, Stephen 'Rosa'			695				
2439	Lynch, Stephen (Capt)						5	1
2488	Lynch, Stephen	c 1675		2487				
1277	Lynch, Stephen (Mayor)		1531	1275	??? Bodkin	1518	3	1
670	Lynch, Stephen (Mayor)		15 Aug 1579	672			2	1
1878	Lynch, Stephen Blosse	1819	12 Oct 1896	1869				
1554	Lynch, Stephen fitz				Eleanor Browne	c 1655	1	1
1540	Lynch, Stephen fitz				Joan Browne		3	1
2654	Lynch, Sybil			2643	Roy Gowthorpe	1918	1	1
1285	Lynch, Thomas			695			1	1
1315	Lynch, Thomas	1646	on/bef 1712	1303	Eleanor Martin	20 Sep 1670	3	2
1337	Lynch, Thomas	4 Apr 1707		1322	Julia Hamilton	11 Feb 1740	2	1
1392	Lynch, Thomas		10 Aug 1872	1369	Rosina Tighe	14 Jul 1828	5	1
1412	Lynch, Thomas			1392				
1415	Lynch, Thomas		Mar 1905	1407				
1470	Lynch, Thomas			1464	Eleanor O'Brien		1	1
1495	Lynch, Thomas			1486	Margaret French		2	1
1593	Lynch, Thomas			1506				
1704	Lynch, Thomas			1611				
2070	Lynch, Thomas						2	1
2072	Lynch, Thomas			2070				
2073	Lynch, Thomas		c 1798	1868	??? Browne	1782	4	1
2077	Lynch, Thomas			2073				
2093	Lynch, Thomas			2087				
2099	Lynch, Thomas			2076	Mary Leonard	30 Jul 1841		1
2282	Lynch, Thomas			2267				
2287	Lynch, Thomas			2267				
2594	Lynch, Thomas			2573	Honoria Jordan		1	1
2817	Lynch, Thomas						1	1
2889	Lynch, Thomas			825				
2921	Lynch, Thomas				Cecilia Browne			1
2937	Lynch, Thomas				Eleanor Skerrett		1	1
2944	Lynch, Thomas		Apr 1897	2593			1	1
2992	Lynch, Thomas			2989				
569	Lynch, Thomas			564				
589	Lynch, Thomas			582				
678	Lynch, Thomas			680			1	1
691	Lynch, Thomas			688	Mary 'Maria' Athy		1	1
695	Lynch, Thomas		1419?	693			7	3
1481	Lynch, Thomas 'de'			2104			1	1
682	Lynch, Thomas 'de'			684			1	1
686	Lynch, Thomas 'de'			1479	Bridget Marshal	1280	3	1
2560	Lynch, Thomas 'Tom'	c.1913		1443				
2772	Lynch, Thomas (BL)			1058			2	1
855	Lynch, Thomas (Mayor)			579				
1296	Lynch, Thomas ?		1652	1294	Margaret Blake		10	2
2827	Lynch, Thomas ?			1296	Catherine Blake		1	1
1682	Lynch, Thomas D Wilson	1870	4 May 1947	1681	Henrietta K. Joyce	1901	2	1
2712	Lynch, Thomas Harvey			2707				
1877	Lynch, Thomas Ker B.	1818	Dec 1891	1869				
1505	Lynch, Thomas Michel	1710	1783	1502	Elizabeth Drouillard	May 1740	8	2
1578	Lynch, Thomas Michel	May 1754	13 Aug 1840	1505	Elizabeth Davies	c 1821		1
1628	Lynch, Ventura 'y Z.			1617			1	1
1288	Lynch, Walter			1286				

Num	Name	Birth date	Died	Father	Spouse	Married	Ch	M
3044	Lynch, Walter			729				
886	Lynch, Walter			695				
908	Lynch, Walter 'de'			686				
2377	Lynch, Walter (Bishop)	abt 1595	14 Jul 1663/68	2376				
1271	Lynch, William		1492	885	Catherine French		1	1
1460	Lynch, William			1296	Mary Burke		1	1
1609	Lynch, William			1607	Catherine Blake		1	1
1703	Lynch, William			1611				
2289	Lynch, William			2267	??? Skerrett			1
2864	Lynch, William						1	1
2912	Lynch, William		bef Feb 1761				1	1
659	Lynch, William			579			3	1
661	Lynch, William			659				
721	Lynch, William			717				
688	Lynch, William 'de'			686	Anne '. O'Halloran		2	1
713	Lynch, William ? Ulick	abt 1536	abt 1614/c.78y	705	Simona Fleming		2	1
885	Lynch, William Black		c.1476	693			1	1
929	Lynch, William C.	Mar 1826	21 Dec 1863	847				
1305	Lynch, William fitz						3	2
1730	Lynch, William fitz							
1906	Lynch, William Joseph	1835	1874	1684				
2859	Lynch, William Michael	c.1811	21 Jan 1841	1869				
1903	Lynch, William Patk	29 Sep 1871		1681	Marie B. Maguire	25 Nov 1925		1
758	Lynch, Winifred			729				
900	Lynch-Blosse, Alice			898	Robert Arthur Milne	27 Sep 1934	1	1
3068	Lynch-Blosse, Blair	1974		3065				
3035	Lynch-Blosse, Bridget	10 Feb 1958		986	Peter James Barry	9 Dec 2000	2	1
3075	Lynch-Blosse, Caroline	22 Aug 1951		986				
958	Lynch-Blosse, C.	c.1821	24 Nov 1915/94	847				
853	Lynch-Blosse, C.			843				
994	Lynch-Blosse, C.	1983		990				
3080	Lynch-Blosse, Cecil	4 Dec 1890		980	Dorothy Delahaize	31 Oct 1915	1	1
2900	Lynch-Blosse, C.	c.1802		843				
852	Lynch-Blosse, C.			843				1
3078	Lynch-Blosse, C.			3076	Leonard Arthur Bate	7 Dec 1918		1
3067	Lynch-Blosse, Craig	1967		3065				
986	Lynch-Blosse, David	24 Nov 1925	15 Oct 1971	982	Elizabeth '. Payne	8 Mar 1950	3	1
3084	Lynch-Blosse, David	14 Jan 1950		3082	Nadine Baddeley	1989	1	1
3082	Lynch-Blosse, E Hugh	30 Jul 1917	25 Feb 2000	3080	Jean E. Robertson	27 Mar 1946	1	1
980	Lynch-Blosse, Edward F	25 Dec 1853	1926	959	Edith C. Walker	11 Dec 1883	5	1
832	Lynch-Blosse, Francis			818	Hatton Smith		2	1
957	Lynch-Blosse, Francis	Dec 1831	26 Jul 1864	847				
847	Lynch-Blosse, Francis	Aug 1801	1840	843	Elizabeth Plunkett	Mar 1824	4	1
905	Lynch-Blosse, Francis	27 Nov 1868	17 Feb 1915	874				
3076	Lynch-Blosse, Francis	28 Apr 1859	1 Jun 1926	959	Emily Vivian Cory	15 Dec 1885	1	1
3061	Lynch-Blosse, G Robert	1895		980	Lucy Myra Adams		1	1
3065	Lynch-Blosse, Gerald	1936	2005	3061	Moira Jean Johns		2	1
995	Lynch-Blosse, Hannah V	1985		990				
906	Lynch-Blosse, Harriet	25 May 1862	14 Jan 1942	874	Henry A Robinson	6 Nov 1883	1	1
982	Lynch-Blosse, Hely R.	6 Sep 1887	21 Apr 1928	980	Evangeline Hudson	25 Apr 1922	1	1
896	Lynch-Blosse, Henry	21 Apr 1857	17 Aug 1918	874	Annie Stokes	Apr 1881		1
975	Lynch-Blosse, Henry	29 Oct 1884	17 May 1969	980	Cicely Edith Bircham	17 Feb 1914		1
830	Lynch-Blosse, Henry	14 Oct 1749	1788 dspl	818	Sibella Cottle		8	2
959	Lynch-Blosse, Henry	11 Feb 1813	28 Jan 1879	843	Charlotte F. Knight	16 Jul 1844	4	1
979	Lynch-Blosse, Henry	20 Jan 1852	18 Jan 1896	959				
848	Lynch-Blosse, Mary	c.1802		843	Robert Plunkett	27 Mar 1830		1
878	Lynch-Blosse, Mary C.	3 Jul 1865	25 Aug 1955/90	874	Robert N. Hardinge	8 Mar 1892		1
3086	Lynch-Blosse, Oliver	12 Nov 1989		3084				
3063	Lynch-Blosse, Patrick	11 Apr 1900	Jun 1942	980	Beatrice Laughrane			1
990	Lynch-Blosse, Richard	26 Aug 1953		986	Cara L. Sutherland	18 Sep 1976	2	2
874	Lynch-Blosse, Robert	15 Feb 1825	3 Dec 1893/68y	847	Harriet Browne	31 Mar 1853	6	1
898	Lynch-Blosse, Robert	14 Feb 1861	23 Jun 1942	874	Alice Pery-Knox-Gore	27 Nov 1893	1	1
967	Lynch-Blosse, Robert	17 Jan 1887	4 Jul 1951	963	Dorothy Mary Owen	25 Apr 1911	1	2

Num	Name	Birth date	Died	Father	Spouse	Married	Ch	M
971	Lynch-Blosse, Robert	1 Apr 1915	21 Apr 1963	967				
843	Lynch-Blosse, Robert	Feb 1784	Jan 1818	832	Elizabeth Gorman	8 Sep 1800	8	2
963	Lynch-Blosse, Robert	5 Aug 1848	13 Jul 1933	959	Mary C. Walker	6 Dec 1881	1	1
904	Lynch-Blosse, William	15 Feb 1864	19 Nov 1870	874				
2883	Lynch-Robinson, C.	1884	1958	907				
1962	Lynch-Staunton, Alfred	1859		1957				
1983	Lynch-Staunton, Alice			1956				
1975	Lynch-Staunton, Anna			1915				
1982	Lynch-Staunton, C.	1854		1956				
1976	Lynch-Staunton, E.			1915				
1974	Lynch-Staunton, Fanny			1915				
1957	Lynch-Staunton, F.	1828		1915	Victoire Corbet	1857	2	1
1961	Lynch-Staunton, George	1858		1957				1
1920	Lynch-Staunton, George			1916	Margaret Kirkpatrick	1870	1	1
1915	Lynch-Staunton, George	1798	4 Apr 1882	1547	Sarah Jane Hardwick	1824	10	1
1916	Lynch-Staunton, Henry	1801		1547	Charlotte Brock Wood	1838	1	1
1924	Lynch-Staunton, Henry			1920	Helen Grace	27 Apr 1907		1
1977	Lynch-Staunton, Lucy			1915				
1956	Lynch-Staunton, Marcus	1826	19 Oct 1896	1915	Horatia Rushworth	1851	2	1
1967	Lynch-Staunton, Mary			1915	John Blake	1861		1
1963	Lynch-Staunton, R.	1846		1915	Marion Duncan			1
1978	Lynch-Staunton, Sarah			1915				
1973	Lynch-Staunton, V.		1857	1915				
189	Lyons, Bridget C.	c.1872	12 Nov 1931/59		Patrick McHugh	c.1913		1
110	Lyons, Mary	c 1881		381	Thaddeus '. McHugh	19 Feb 1905	7	1
381	Lyons, Thomas				Margaret Varley		1	1
2043	MacDonnell, Bridget			2044	Philip Edmond Athy		4	1
2044	MacDonnell, Randle						1	1
1798	MacMurrough, Aoife			1804	Richard S. Clare	1170	1	1
1804	MacMurrough, Dermot						1	1
2401	MacWilliam, Richard						1	1
799	Madden, Anthony '.				Bridget Lynch			1
3031	Maguire, Constantine						1	1
3029	Maguire, Marie Blanche			3031	Clement I. Ryan			2
2617	Mahon, Margaret				Andrew Lynch	1741	5	1
3072	Mahon, Ross	1725	17 Mar 1788		Anne Browne	12 Oct 1762		1
475	Malone, ???						1	1
424	Malone, Bartley	c 1850		475	Mary Naughton	7 Dec 1876	1	1
423	Malone, Bridget	c.1901	7 Mar 1968/67y	424	Michael Walsh	6 Oct 1937	1	1
2216	Manning, Mary	c 1747			Hugh Evans		1	1
1568	Mannion, Mary Anne				Peter (Sir) Lynch		4	1
1636	March, Aleida				Che 'de la Guevara			1
1280	Mares, Janet			1269	John Bodkin		1	1
1269	Mares, John				Christina Lynch		1	1
1816	Margaret, Princess			1817	Gilbert Marshal	Aug 1235		1
1891	Marryott, E S (Col)				Elizabeth Lynch			1
1791	Marshal, Anselm			1793			1	1
1803	Marshal, Anselm		Dec 1245	1795	Maud 'de' Bohun			1
1846	Marshal, Bridget			1785	Thomas 'de' Lynch	1280	3	1
1837	Marshal, Eve/Eva		1246	1795	William 'de' Braose	bef 1219		1
1801	Marshal, Gilbert (Sir)		27 Jun 1241	1795	Margaret Lanvallei	Sep 1230		2
1844	Marshal, Hawisa			1842	Robert (Sir) Morlee			1
1814	Marshal, Isabel			1795	Gilbert (Earl) Clare	9 Oct 1217	1	1
1839	Marshal, Joan '.		aft 1234	1795	Warin 'de' Munchensi	aft 1220		1
1787	Marshal, John		1235	1791	Aliva 'de' Rie		2	1
1841	Marshal, John		1242	1787				
1843	Marshal, John		1316	1842				
1793	Marshal, John the				Sibyl of Salisbury		2	1
1826	Marshal, Maude Matilda	bef 1194	1245	1795	Hugh (Earl N. Bigod	1206	1	1
1800	Marshal, Richard		16 Apr 1234	1795	Gervase 'de' Dinan	bef 1224		1
1835	Marshal, Sibilla		aft 1238	1795	William Ferrers	bef 1219		1
1802	Marshal, Walter		24 Nov 1245	1795	Margaret 'de' Quenci	2 Jan 1242		1
1785	Marshal, William		bef Jun 1280	1787			2	1

Num	Name	Birth date	Died	Father	Spouse	Married	Ch	M
1799	Marshal, William	c.1190-91	6 Apr 1231	1795	Alice 'de' Bethune	Sep 1214		2
1842	Marshal, William	c 1277	1314	879			2	1
1795	Marshal, William (Sir)	c 1146	14 May 1219	1793	Isabel 'de' Clare	1189	10	1
879	Marshall, Lord John?		1282	1785			1	1
1276	Martin, Anastacia				Dominick '. Lynch		7	1
2219	Martin, Annabel '.	c 1710	28 Sep 1766	2177				
2227	Martin, Annabel '.	abt 1688		2175	Edmond Fitzpatrick		1	2
2177	Martin, Anthony	1684	15 May 1748	2175	Bridget Kirwan	c 1707	4	1
2199	Martin, Anthony Crosby	1 Apr 1771	21 Aug 1846	2181	Marie l'Espinasse	5 Oct 1806		1
2220	Martin, Bridget	c 1712		2177	Morgan McNamara			1
2207	Martin, Charles		late 1800	2185				
2871	Martin, Christian '.			2975	Martin Darcy		2	1
2226	Martin, Christina	abt 1686		2175				
2238	Martin, Edward	30 Oct 1834		2190	Mariana M. Counsell	2 Dec 1862		1
1290	Martin, Eleanor			1452	Andrew Lynch		3	1
1316	Martin, Eleanor			1317	Thomas Lynch	20 Sep 1670	3	1
2229	Martin, Elizabeth	abt 1694		2175				
666	Martin, Elizabeth	abt 1575	bef 1639	668	James 'Rivagh' Darcy		11	?
1698	Martin, Elizabeth '.			1699	George Staunton		1	1
2236	Martin, Evan Stratford	26 Oct 1826		2190	Anne Blackeney	9 Nov 1859		1
2246	Martin, Frederick O.	5 Sep 1832		2190	Catherine Blackeney	1 Jan 1862		1
2208	Martin, Georgina T.	23 Nov 1806	11 Feb 1840	2185				
2204	Martin, Harriet	5 Jul 1801	12 Jan 1891	2185				
2172	Martin, James			2165	Mary Darcy			1
1699	Martin, James 'Martyn'						1	1
2230	Martin, Jane	abt 1696	1730	2175	James Darcy			2
2164	Martin, Jasper		1629	2163			1	1
2166	Martin, Jasper		1710	2165			1	1
1452	Martin, John ? Thomas						1	1
2240	Martin, John Robert	22 Feb 1825		2190	Sophia Stimpson	27 Sep 1855		2
2188	Martin, Laetitia	Feb 1785	23 Apr 1858	2185	Charles Peshall	8 May 1808		1
2228	Martin, Margaret	abt 1692		2175	Martin Blake			1
1545	Martin, Margery				Stephen Burke	c.1760	1	1
2111	Martin, Mary			2225	Thomas (4th Blake	1649		1
2202	Martin, Mary	c 1755	1813	2181	Patrick Darcy	4 Nov 1775		1
2223	Martin, Mary	abt 1685		2175	Patrick Kirwan	c.1703		1
2347	Martin, Mary				Timothy O'Flaherty	abt 1646	1	1
2210	Martin, Mary Jane	18 Dec 1810	15 Apr 1893	2185				
2209	Martin, Mary L '.	28 Aug 1815	30 Oct 1850	2189	Arthur Gonne Bell	14 Sep 1847		1
1721	Martin, Mathew							
2167	Martin, Nicholas		1731	2166	Jane French			2
2403	Martin, Peter 'Piers'				Mary 'Marie' Lynch			1
1935	Martin, Richard				Lucy Lynch			1
2179	Martin, Richard	c 1708	bef Sep 1768	2177	Mable 'Sweet' Kelly			1
2225	Martin, Richard			2163	Margaret French		1	1
2244	Martin, Richard	11 Aug 1823	29 Oct 1886	2190	Elizabeth Cunningham	9 Jul 1858		1
2975	Martin, Richard						1	1
2185	Martin, Richard '.	Feb 1754	6 Jan 1834	2181	Elizabeth Vesey	Feb 1777	8	2
2175	Martin, Richard '.	c 1655	bef May 1731	2165	Catherine French	c 1681	8	1
668	Martin, Richard						2	1
2190	Martin, Richard (Rev)	25 Mar 1797	4 Apr 1878	2185	Emily Sylvia Kirwan	6 Dec 1821	7	1
2165	Martin, Robert			2164			3	1
2181	Martin, Robert	c.1714	7 Aug 1794	2177	Bridget Barnewall	6 Apr 1753	4	2
761	Martin, Robert				Judith Lynch			1
2176	Martin, Robert 'Robin'	abt 1682	1705	2175				
2196	Martin, Robert (Capt)	19 Mar 1770	20 May 1840	2181	Mary O'Flaherty	5 Oct 1806		1
2163	Martin, Robert (Mayor)		1621	668			2	1
2211	Martin, St George	1788	1802/14y	2185				
2248	Martin, Therese	9 Sep 1822		2190				
3048	Martin, Thomas (Dr)				Ellis Lynch	bef 1714		1
2189	Martin, Thomas B (MP)	4 Oct 1786	23 Apr 1847	2185	Julia Kirwan	14 Feb 1814	1	1
1317	Martin, Thomas fitz						1	1
1383	Martin, Walter				Julia Lynch	1800		1

An extract from the database of 2843 individuals (1 October 2013) including the Anglo-Norman Lynches who settled in Galway and members of my extended family (PaulBMcNulty.com on http://www.myfamily) (Ch = number of children; M = number of marriages).

Num	Name	Birth date	Died	Father	Spouse	Married	Ch	M
854	Marylski, Blanche de ?		18 May 1908	1242	Marcus N. Lynch	1867	5	1
1242	Marylski, Julius							1
380	Mason, Bartholomew '.				Annie Griffin			1
2999	Maxwell, Catherine				George (Capt) Moore		1	1
466	McArthur, Christobel				Seamus Fallon			1
2132	McCarty, Donough (1st				Eleanor Butler		1	1
2131	McCarty, Helen			2132	William (7th Burke		1	1
58	McCauley, Owen				Anne 'Annie' ZZ?		1	1
23	McCauley, Susan	c 1833	24 Jan 1903	58	Charles McNulty	10 Oct 1875		1
196	McColgan, ???	c 1770					3	1
200	McColgan, ???			194	??? McCormick		3	1
198	McColgan, Daniel			196				
199	McColgan, James			196				
194	McColgan, John	c.1806	12 Jan 1875/69	196	Hannah ZZ?	c.1830	2	1
193	McColgan, Maria	c.1832	3 Jan 1871/39y	194	Charles McNulty	c.1862	1	1
362	McCormack, ??? ?				Winifred Fallon			1
201	McCormick, ???				??? McColgan		3	1
204	McCormick, Catherine			201				
202	McCormick, John George			201				1
203	McCormick, Mary J.			201				
2884	McDermot, Margaret				Henry Lynch-Blosse		1	1
541	McDonagh, ???	c 1805					1	1
1208	McDonagh, Anne 'Annie'			1209	Patrick Fallon	6 Jun 1895		1
62	McDonagh, Anne 'Nan	20 Jul 1912	21 Jul 1985/73	68	Patrick '. Conneely	c.1935	8	1
66	McDonagh, Barbara '.	c.1830		529	Learai S. Conneely	bef 1854	5	1
3119	McDonagh, Bartley			529				
533	McDonagh, Bidm ?	c 1795					1	1
1214	McDonagh, Bridget							
187	McDonagh, Colman '.				Mary ZZ?		1	1
1082	McDonagh, Edmond ? '.							
529	McDonagh, Edmond ? '.	c 1795					6	1
75	McDonagh, Honor 'Nora	c 1840		541	Beartla '. Conneely	c.1861	5	1
68	McDonagh, James 'Rua'	1869	4 Dec 1925	72	Anne 'Nan T. Toole	c.1902	2	1
183	McDonagh, John			182	Mary Harte		2	1
186	McDonagh, John			183				
1080	McDonagh, Joseph							
185	McDonagh, Martin			183				
72	McDonagh, Martin 'Rua'	c.1831	c.1903/c.72y	533	Honor Flaherty	2 Nov 1856	1	1
3117	McDonagh, Maureen			529				
182	McDonagh, Michael			187	Margaret Conneely		1	1
3121	McDonagh, Michael '.			529				
3109	McDonagh, Nora	7 Dec 1906	15 Mar 1989	68	John Walsh	9 Apr 1939	1	1
1084	McDonagh, Pat							
3120	McDonagh, Patrick '.			529				
3118	McDonagh, Redmond '.			529				
1209	McDonagh, Walter		bef 1895				1	1
2951	McDonald, ??? ?				Elizabeth '. Lynch			1
2705	McDonnell, James				??? Lynch			1
801	McDonnell, Joseph				Mary Lynch			1
1012	McDonnell, Maria				Thomas (Dr) Bodkin	16 May 1843	2	1
2741	McDonnell, Myles				Catherine Lynch			1
3137	McDonough, Deborah '.			3135				
3135	McDonough, James '.			3131	? ZZ?		1	1
3131	McDonough, James Jos	6 Apr 1903		3123	Mary ZZ?		2	1
3123	McDonough, James Jos				Mary 'Maire Conneely		1	1
3133	McDonough, Mary			3131	Richard '. Kacin			1
455	McGarry, Eileen		c. Aug 2001		John Fallon		1	1
474	McGuire, Mary	c.1833	24 Apr 1910/77		Patrick Grealish	29 Jan 1855	8	1
1055	McHugh, 'Boy'			1052			1	1
397	McHugh, ???						1	1
46	McHugh, Agnes	c 1909	c 1909	12				
176	McHugh, Alison Mai			174				
48	McHugh, Anne (Sr C.	25 Jul 1912	6 Jul 2005	12				

An extract from the database of 2843 individuals (1 October 2013) including the Anglo-Norman Lynches who settled in Galway and members of my extended family (PaulBMcNulty.com on http://www.myfamily) (Ch = number of children; M = number of marriages).

Num	Name	Birth date	Died	Father	Spouse	Married	Ch	M
156	McHugh, Anne Marie			50	William Cleere	c.1978	2	1
2536	McHugh, Anthony 'Tony'				Gerarda Lynch		2	1
208	McHugh, Barbara			108				
147	McHugh, Barbara Ann			123				
146	McHugh, Caitlin M.			144				
178	McHugh, Conor			174				
2538	McHugh, Deirdre			2536				
1050	McHugh, Edmond ?						1	1
1052	McHugh, Edmond Og			1050			2	1
1216	McHugh, Eileen			84				
1057	McHugh, Erevan ?			1055				
177	McHugh, Eva Juliett			174				
51	McHugh, Evelyn 'Eva'	5 Aug 1922	9 Oct 2004/82y	12	John (Jack) Landy	19 Mar 1977		1
164	McHugh, Evin			161				
165	McHugh, Holly			161				
3001	McHugh, Hugh 'Boy'		c.1701				1	1
113	McHugh, Jerome (Rev)	c 1934		111				
133	McHugh, John	c 1876	21 Oct 1934/58	26				
134	McHugh, John	c 1848		32			3	1
137	McHugh, John			134				1
170	McHugh, John			50	Christabel Gloster	c 1987	2	1
1217	McHugh, John 'Jack'			84				
47	McHugh, John (Bro E.	4 Jul 1911	26 Jun 1995/84	12				
117	McHugh, John (Rev)	c.1936		111				
3	McHugh, Kathleen M	9 Aug 1914	24 Jul 2000/85	12	Thomas B. McNulty	3 Sep 1935	3	1
174	McHugh, Kieran			50	Mary Farrell	26 Jun 1999	4	1
173	McHugh, Lauren			170				
1215	McHugh, Margaret			84				
124	McHugh, Margaret	12 Apr 1906	c. Oct 1906	108				
3002	McHugh, Margaret '.			3001				
115	McHugh, Martha T	c 1937		111	John Hubbard	c 1962		1
83	McHugh, Mary	c.1881	3 Jun 1974/94y	26	Thomas Higgins		3	1
118	McHugh, Mary Agnes	19 Dec 1909	2 Feb 2001	108	Thomas L Harrigan	c 1935	2	1
1054	McHugh, Morogh		c.1601	1052				
120	McHugh, Nora	21 Oct 1917	8 Dec 2001	108	??? Robertson	c.1937		1
140	McHugh, Nora	c 1849		32			1	1
135	McHugh, Patrick			134	Brigid Byrne			1
26	McHugh, Patrick	c 1846	12 Nov 1930/84	32	Bridget Courtney	3 Apr 1875	6	1
85	McHugh, Patrick	c 1883	16 Nov 1949	26	Bridget C. Lyons	c.1913		1
111	McHugh, Patrick H	19 May 1907	11 Jan 1995/87	108	Dorothy Kunsemuller	3 Jul 1933	3	1
1218	McHugh, Peter			84				
141	McHugh, Peter	c 1851		32	??? Hughes			1
84	McHugh, Peter	c.1885	aft 1949	26	Margaret Bergin		4	1
172	McHugh, Rachel			170				
179	McHugh, Robert			174				
163	McHugh, Ruairi			161				1
160	McHugh, Ruth			50				
2537	McHugh, Sinead			2536				
32	McHugh, Thaddeus	c 1800	4 Nov 1893/93y	397	Nora ZZ?		4	1
108	McHugh, Thaddeus 'Tim'	1 Jul 1879	6 Oct 1959	26	Mary Lyons	19 Feb 1905	7	1
12	McHugh, Thomas	1 Oct 1877	9 May 1957/79y	26	Mary Fallon	7 Jan 1909	7	1
161	McHugh, Thomas			50	Geraldine Cleary	22 Sep 1992	3	1
50	McHugh, Thomas F	11 Jul 1919	12 Jun 2001	12	Juliett Bolger	24 Sep 1956	5	1
122	McHugh, Thomas Francis	20 Jul 1914	aft 2000	108				
139	McHugh, Timothy			134			1	1
144	McHugh, Timothy			123	Leilani ZZ?	c 1984	1	1
123	McHugh, Timothy Joseph	16 Jan 1913	12 Jan 1974	108	Barbara R ZZ?		2	1
49	McHugh, Una	28 Oct 1916		12	James '. O'Flaherty	c 1943	4	1
386	McLaughlin, ???	c 1750					2	1
388	McLaughlin, Denis ?			386				
28	McLaughlin, Sophia	c 1781	23 Dec 1873	386	Robert McNulty		1	1
2627	McMahon, Bryan						1	1
2626	McMahon, Thomasina			2627	Charles Lynch	1809		1

An extract from the database of 2843 individuals (1 October 2013) including the Anglo-Norman Lynches who settled in Galway and members of my extended family (PaulBMcNulty.com on http://www.myfamily) (Ch = number of children; M = number of marriages).

Num	Name	Birth date	Died	Father	Spouse	Married	Ch	M
2334	McMorrishe, Mary				Geoffrey Browne		3	1
2808	McMullen, Anne				Charles John Lynch	c.1821		1
2115	McNamara, Dorothea			2117	David Comyn	8 Feb 1762	1	1
2235	McNamara, Morgan				Bridget Martin			1
2117	McNamara, William				Catherine Sarsfield		1	1
38	McNulty, Ailbhe			36				
22	McNulty, Charles	c.1815	1 Jan 1886/74y	27	Maria McColgan	c.1862	1	2
40	McNulty, Charles J.	c 1895	5 Apr 1947	4				
19	McNulty, Dara			1				
36	McNulty, Hugh			2	Emer Gillen	27 Dec 1980	2	1
384	McNulty, Hugh ?	c 1750	c 1840				1	1
37	McNulty, Jennifer			36				
41	McNulty, John	12 Sep 1898	4 Jun 1966	4				
42	McNulty, Margaret M	5 Nov 1900	17 Jun 1966	4				
21	McNulty, Meabh			1				
20	McNulty, Nora '.			1				
35	McNulty, Patricia M	23 Sep 1936		2				
1	McNulty, Paul Bernard	22 Mar 1940		2	'Treasa '. Conneely	21 Sep 1974	3	1
27	McNulty, Robert	c.1780	3 Jan 1874/94y	384	Sophia McLaughlin		1	1
4	McNulty, Thomas	1 Sep 1863	8 Nov 1903/40y	22	Mary Boylan	30 Dec 1891	4	1
2	McNulty, Thomas B.	25 Jan 1897	19 Oct 1960	4	Kathleen M McHugh	3 Sep 1935	3	1
2486	Meade, Judith				Isidore Lynch			1
337	Melody, Maria							
336	Melody, Michael							
807	Merrick, ???				Elizabeth '. Lynch			1
3164	Miles, ZZ?				Cece O'Reardon			1
901	Milne, Robert Arthur				Alice Lynch-Blosse	27 Sep 1934	1	1
3074	Milne, Robert Cecil	5 Nov 1935		901				
1529	Moffitt, Francis				Alice Crean-Lynch	1809-10		1
3090	Monaghan, Bridget			3087			1	1
3089	Monaghan, Catherine			3087				
3088	Monaghan, Martin			3087				
3087	Monaghan, Michael				Mary Ann Farrell		3	1
1028	Mooney, Frances ?				Joseph R Cox			1
3004	Moore, ???						4	1
3012	Moore, ???			3004			1	1
803	Moore, ???				Catherine Lynch			1
2925	Moore, ??? 'More'				Mary 'Maria' Burke		2	1
3169	Moore, Augustus			1989			1	1
2526	Moore, Cresacre 'More'	1534	1607	2528	Elizabeth Gage		1	1
3107	Moore, Edmund	c.1731		2001				
3005	Moore, Ellinor			3004	??? Atkinson			1
3052	Moore, Garrett		1723	812				
3003	Moore, Garrett (Col)		1704 osp	3004	Margaret or Burke			1
1990	Moore, George	1773?	1840	1994	Louisa Browne	Sep 1807	1	1
1994	Moore, George	1729	Nov 1799	2001	Catherine Killikelly	c 1765	3	1
2524	Moore, George				Maria Pryce		1	1
2525	Moore, George (Capt)				Catherine Maxwell		1	1
2437	Moore, George Augustus	1852	1933	1989				
1989	Moore, George Henry	19 Apr 1810		1990	Mary Blake	1851	4	1
2927	Moore, Gerard 'Gerardo			2925				
2926	Moore, Joan 'Joanne			2925			1	1
2001	Moore, John			2524	Jane Athy	c.1727	3	1
2529	Moore, John 'More'	1509	1547	2531	Anne Cresacre		1	1
2532	Moore, John 'More'	c.1451	1530				1	1
2000	Moore, John	1767?	6 Dec 1799/36?	1994				
812	Moore, John ?		1706	3012			2	1
3007	Moore, Mary			3004	??? Garvey			1
811	Moore, Mary		c.1784	812	Marcus French		6	2
3168	Moore, Maurice '.			1989				
3157	Moore, Nina Louisa M.			1989	??? Kilkelly		1	1
3105	Moore, Peter	c.1766		1994				
3170	Moore, Peter			3169				

Num	Name	Birth date	Died	Father	Spouse	Married	Ch	M
3106	Moore, Robert	c.1728		2001				
2528	Moore, Thomas 'More'	1531	1606	2529	Mary Scrope		1	1
3150	Moore, Thomas 'More'	1607	1666	2526	Mary Brooke		1	2
3152	Moore, Thomas 'More'	1635		3150			1	1
2531	Moore, Thomas 'More'	1478	1535	2532	Johanna 'Joan, Colt		1	1
1192	Moran, Michael							
2990	Morgan, Mary				John Brown Lynch		6	1
1845	Morlee, Robert (Sir)				Hawisa Marshal			1
1166	Morris, Catherine							
1089	Morris, James	1845		360				
1039	Morris, John	c.1726	c.1749	1040				
360	Morris, John	c.1819	8 Sep 1852/33y		Julia Fallon	16 Jan 1842	3	1
1091	Morris, Mary	1847		360				
2747	Morris, Mary				Ignatius Lynch		1	1
1092	Morris, Michael							
1044	Morris, Morgan			1042				
1045	Morris, Morgan			1040				
1231	Morris, Morgan							
1040	Morris, Patrick	c 1690					3	1
1134	Morris, Patrick 'Patt'	1844		360				
1042	Morris, Thomas		c.1822	1040	Sebina ZZ?		1	1
1096	Morris, Thomas							
1081	Mullin, Agnes							
1840	Munchensi, Warin 'de'		1255		Joan '. Marshal	aft 1220		1
408	Murphy, Mary ?				??? Bolger		1	1
1151	Murphy, Mary Jane		19 Jul 1898		John Stephen Kearney			1
290	Nally, Angela				Vincent C O'Brien		3	1
477	Naughton, ???						1	1
425	Naughton, Mary	c 1856		477	Bartley Malone	7 Dec 1876	1	1
706	Neale, Catherine			707	Marcus Lynch		1	1
707	Neale, John				Catherine Penrise		1	1
3162	Neary, Mary				John O'Reardon		1	1
1357	Nolan, ???				Winifred Burke			1
2854	Nolan, Thomas				Mary Lynch			1
1032	Norman, ???				Emma Bodkin			1
1017	Norman, Francis ?			1018	Margaret ZZ?		1	1
1018	Norman, John ?						1	1
1582	Nort, R.		aft 1783		Thomas Michel Lynch	Oct 1768	2	1
2037	Nottingham, ???			2038	Edmond Lynch Athy		2	1
2038	Nottingham, Peter						1	1
2585	Nugent, Helena Mary	c.1855		2586	Richard C. Lynch	20 Jan 1876	1	1
2586	Nugent, John (Sir)	1800	1859				1	1
1433	Nugent, Oliver			1434	Bridget Lynch			1
1434	Nugent, Walter (Col)						1	1
292	O'Brien, Aedeen	c 1980		288				
15	O'Brien, Anne	c 1845	22 Jan 1917/73	16	John Fallon	26 Sep 1868	10	1
1079	O'Brien, B 'Bridget'?							
289	O'Brien, Cathal			288				
1177	O'Brien, Catherine							
16	O'Brien, Charles	c 1786	29 Sep 1875	395	Mary Fahy	c 1833	2	1
286	O'Brien, Christopher			282	Nora Carroll		1	1
1737	O'Brien, Conor						1	1
1471	O'Brien, Eleanor			1472	Thomas Lynch		1	1
291	O'Brien, Flan	c.1978		288				
922	O'Brien, Frances			923	Hyacinth Darcy		1	1
1736	O'Brien, Helen			1737	Roger O'Shaughnessy	1688	1	1
1472	O'Brien, Henry						1	1
923	O'Brien, Henry						1	1
1186	O'Brien, Honor							
1751	O'Brien, Honor '.			1753	Roger O'Shaughnessy		4	1
282	O'Brien, Joseph			280	Catherine Clancy		2	1
2873	O'Brien, Julia				Patrick French		2	1
2563	O'Brien, Julia 'Julie'	c.1872		280	Michael O'Brien	c.1895	1	1

Num	Name	Birth date	Died	Father	Spouse	Married	Ch	M
2343	O'Brien, Margaret			1753	Richard (2nd Burke	24 Nov 1553	3	1
2565	O'Brien, Mary	c.1897		2564	John Cooke	c.1915	3	1
2564	O'Brien, Michael				Julia '. O'Brien	c.1895	1	1
280	O'Brien, Michael	c 1835		16	Mary Cunningham	4 Feb 1869	2	1
395	O'Brien, Michael ?						1	1
1753	O'Brien, Murrough (1st				Eleanor Fitzgerald		2	2
2411	O'Brien, Teige				Joan O'Shaughnessy	aft 1625		1
288	O'Brien, Vincent C	c 1940		286	Angela Nally		3	1
284	O'Brien, William			282	Molly Heffernan			1
2398	O'Carroll, Grace '.			2399	Ulick (1st E. Burke		1	1
2399	O'Carroll, Mulroy						1	1
1229	O'Connell, ???				??? Fallon		1	1
1230	O'Connell, Anne '.	c 1894		1229				
952	O'Connor, Arthur 'O				Catherine Blake	Mar 1853		1
2318	O'Connor, Charles						1	1
2351	O'Connor, Conor 'Og'						1	1
2776	O'Connor, Dermot				Alice Lynch			1
2350	O'Connor, Margaret			2351	Owen '. O'Malley		1	1
2317	O'Connor, Maud			2318	Theobold (1st Burke		1	1
301	O'Donaghy, Bridget ?							
2434	O'Donnell, Elizabeth			2435	Richard Blake		2	1
1240	O'Donnell, Jeremiah							
2435	O'Donnell, Manus (Col)						2	1
2436	O'Donnell, Mary			2435	Marcus 'Mark' Blake		1	1
2388	O'Flaherty, ???				Edward Tyrell			1
2390	O'Flaherty, ???			2391	Roderick O'Flaherty	1652	2	1
2497	O'Flaherty, ???			2498	Dominick Browne		2	1
167	O'Flaherty, Antoinette			150	Glen Ryder	c 1982		2
752	O'Flaherty, Bibyan			753	Peter Lynch		2	1
2331	O'Flaherty, Brian '.	bef 1655		2335	Mabel Browne	1681	3	1
2337	O'Flaherty, Brian '.	1586	1633	2340	F? 'Bourke' Burke		1	1
2359	O'Flaherty, Brian '.			2327				
2328	O'Flaherty, Brian B.			2331	Cecilia French	Apr 1707	1	1
2354	O'Flaherty, Donal		aft 1593	2325				
2324	O'Flaherty, Donal '.		1560	2352	Grace O'Malley	1546	3	1
2360	O'Flaherty, Edmund		May 1653	2327				
2323	O'Flaherty, Flania				David Burke		1	1
151	O'Flaherty, Geraldine			150				
2352	O'Flaherty, Gilleduff						1	1
1085	O'Flaherty, Honor '.							
2358	O'Flaherty, Hugh			2327				
2299	O'Flaherty, Hugh '.		20 Oct 1631		Elizabeth Darcy	1626	1	1
150	O'Flaherty, James '.				Una McHugh	c 1943	4	1
2349	O'Flaherty, John			2331				
2198	O'Flaherty, John (Sir)	1728	1808	2305	Mary Royse	18 Jul 1764	1	1
2326	O'Flaherty, Margaret	abt 1549		2324	Richard D. Burke			1
2197	O'Flaherty, Mary			2198	Robert (Capt) Martin	5 Oct 1806		1
2344	O'Flaherty, Mary			2345				
166	O'Flaherty, Mary Rose			150				
535	O'Flaherty, Matthew	c 1800					1	1
2232	O'Flaherty, Michael	abt 1684		2298	Annabel '. Martin			1
2391	O'Flaherty, Murchadh			2392			1	1
2305	O'Flaherty, Murrough	aft 1707	1760	2328	Joan or Jane Burke	28 Aug 1727	1	1
2348	O'Flaherty, Murrough			2331				
2327	O'Flaherty, Murrough	abt 1552	Apr 1626	2324	Honora '. Burke		8	1
2345	O'Flaherty, Murrough						1	1
2355	O'Flaherty, Murrough		1666	2327	Margaret '. Burke			1
2392	O'Flaherty, Murrough						1	1
2498	O'Flaherty, Murrough						1	1
2335	O'Flaherty, Murrough		aft 1656	2337	Honora '. Burke		1	1
2325	O'Flaherty, Owen	1547	1586	2324	Catherine '. Burke		1	1
2361	O'Flaherty, Patrick			2327				
152	O'Flaherty, Pauline			150	David Poole	1974	4	1

Num	Name	Birth date	Died	Father	Spouse	Married	Ch	M
2298	O'Flaherty, Roderick	1629	abt 1717	2299	??? O'Flaherty	1652	2	1
2356	O'Flaherty, Sara			2327				1
753	O'Flaherty, Timothy	1587		2340	Mary Martin	abt 1646	1	1
2340	O'Flaherty, Timothy		1589		Catherine or Burke		2	1
2373	O'Flaherty, Timothy			2327				
2357	O'Flaherty, Una			2327				
2558	O'Grady, ???				Maud Lynch			1
881	O'Halloran, Anne '.				William 'de' Lynch		2	1
1997	O'Kelly, Helen			1998	Dominick Killikelly		1	1
1998	O'Kelly, John						1	1
2320	O'Malley, Grace	1530	1603	2321	Donal '. O'Flaherty	1546	4	2
90	O'Malley, Mary A '.		25 Nov 1952		Thomas Fallon			1
2321	O'Malley, Owen '.		bef 1575		Margaret O'Connor		1	1
2142	O'Moore, Anne			2143	William Sarsfield		1	1
2143	O'Moore, Rory						1	1
2672	O'Neill, Dermot				Pauline Cooke			1
393	O'Neill, John							
3163	O'Reardon, Cece			3161	ZZ? Miles			1
3161	O'Reardon, John			3160	Mary Neary		1	1
1894	O'Rourke, C (Dr)				Constance E. Lynch			1
367	O'Shaughnessy, ??? '.		bef 1845		Mary Cullinane	c.1830		1
1466	O'Shaughnessy, Charles		1722	1468	Eleanor '. Lynch		1	1
1758	O'Shaughnessy, Darby			1750				
1090	O'Shaughnessy, Darby							
1746	O'Shaughnessy, Dermot		1567	1748			1	1
2396	O'Shaughnessy, Dermot						1	1
1468	O'Shaughnessy, Dermot		1673	1740	Margaret Barry		2	1
1743	O'Shaughnessy, Dermot		8 Jul 1606	1746	Sheila 'Shyly Hubert		2	1
1748	O'Shaughnessy, Dermot						2	1
1465	O'Shaughnessy, Helen			1466	Henry Lynch		1	1
1759	O'Shaughnessy, Joan	bef 1545	1593	1750	Edmond Bermingham	c.1560	1	1
2135	O'Shaughnessy, Joan			2396	William (Sir) Burke		1	2
1752	O'Shaughnessy, John			1750			1	1
1742	O'Shaughnessy, Julia			1740				
1099	O'Shaughnessy, Maria							
1239	O'Shaughnessy, Patrick							
1735	O'Shaughnessy, Roger		11 Jul 1690	1468	Helen O'Brien	1688	1	1
1740	O'Shaughnessy, Roger		c.1650	1743	Elizabeth '. Lynch		2	3
1750	O'Shaughnessy, Roger			1748	Honor '. O'Brien		4	1
1756	O'Shaughnessy, William			1752				
1757	O'Shaughnessy, William		c 1567	1750				
1739	O'Shaughnessy, William		1744	1735				
1745	O'Shaughnessy, William			1743				
2784	O'Vulloghan, Donal '.				Julia '. Fallon	bef 1539		1
2484	Ormsby, John				Mary 'Maria' Lynch		1	1
2007	Ormsby, Oliver			2484	Maria Joyce		2	1
2794	Ormsby, Rebecca			2007	Bryan B. Killikelly			1
2006	Ormsby, Sarah			2007	Philip Lynch			1
1620	Ortiz, Eloisa				Francisco 'y Lynch	1854	1	1
2653	Ottman, Frieda				John Patrick Lynch	7 Dec 1896	3	2
968	Owen, Dorothy Mary		9 Mar 1926	969	Robert Lynch-Blosse	25 Apr 1911	1	1
969	Owen, Edward Cunliffe						1	1
1038	Parker, ???				Anne Bodkin Parker			1
1037	Parker, Anne Bodkin			1021	??? Parker			1
987	Payne, Elizabeth '.	c.1928		988	David Lynch-Blosse	8 Mar 1950	3	1
988	Payne, Thomas Harold						1	1
1483	Penrise, ???						1	1
708	Penrise, Catherine '.			710	John Neale		1	1
1263	Penrise, Joanna			2479	Stephen Lynch		2	1
889	Penrise, Joanna ?			1483	Thomas Lynch		3	1
710	Penrise, Peter 'Piers				Catherine More Athy		1	1
2479	Penrise, Thomas						1	1
1606	Perdiguier, M.				John 'Jean B. Lynch			1

Num	Name	Birth date	Died	Father	Spouse	Married	Ch	M
2649	Perser, Patricia			2647				
899	Pery-Knox-Gore, Alice		25 May 1959	902	Robert Lynch-Blosse	27 Nov 1893	1	1
902	Pery-Knox-Gore, Edmund		1959				1	1
2205	Peshall, Charles	12 Nov 1781		2206	Laetitia Martin	8 May 1808		1
2206	Peshall, John (Sir)				Rebecca Hyde Hall		1	1
868	Plunkett, Elizabeth	c 1801	3 Apr 1885/84y	869	Francis Lynch-Blosse	Mar 1824	4	1
873	Plunkett, Robert (Rev)		1867		Mary Lynch-Blosse	27 Mar 1830		1
869	Plunkett, William C.	1 Jul 1765	4 Jan 1854/89y		Catherine Causland		1	1
210	Poole, Alex			153				
153	Poole, David	1938	18 June 2006		Pauline O'Flaherty	1974	4	1
211	Poole, Garreth			153				
212	Poole, Simon			153				
154	Poole, William			153				
3000	Pryce, Maria				George Moore		1	1
2647	Purser, Arthur (Major)				Beatrice Lynch		3	1
2650	Purser, Mary			2647				
2648	Purser, Ruth			2647				
1819	Quenci, Margaret 'de'		1266	1822	John 'de' Lacy		1	2
1822	Quenci, Robert 'de'				Hawise ZZ?		1	1
2842	Rabbit, Catherine	c.1842	4 Aug 1922/82y		Thomas Cooke		2	1
3166	Reardon, Michelle			3165	ZZ? Kramer			1
3160	Reardon, ZZ?				Ethel Kilkenny		2	1
3165	Reardon, ZZ?			3160			1	1
1672	Redington, Christopher	1780	1825	1668	Frances Dowell	Apr 1812	1	1
1680	Redington, Frances	c.1846	1915	1676	John Wilson Lynch	5 Jul 1865	5	1
1662	Redington, Thomas	c 1700	22 Nov 1780		Margaret Lynch	1719 or 172	1	1
1668	Redington, Thomas	1742	1814	1662	Sarah Burke	1763	1	1
1676	Redington, Thomas N	2 Oct 1815	1862	1672	Anna Eliza Talbot	1842	1	1
2698	Redmond, Henry T.				Margaret Lynch			1
2736	Regan, ???				Henry Michael Lynch			1
849	Richards, Charlotte		5 Oct 1834	850	Robert Lynch-Blosse	13 Mar 1807	3	1
850	Richards, John						1	1
2801	Richardson, Martin				Bridget Lynch			1
1788	Rie, Aliva 'de'			1789	John Marshal		2	1
1789	Rie, Hubert 'de'						1	1
464	Rigney, Padraig				Josephine Fallon			1
121	Robertson, ???				Nora McHugh	c.1937		1
3083	Robertson, Jean Evelyn		26 Nov 2000		E Hugh Lynch-Blosse	27 Mar 1946	1	1
907	Robinson, Henry A (1st	1857	Oct 1927		Harriet Lynch-Blosse	6 Nov 1883	1	1
1036	Robinson, J J				Margaret Bodkin			1
1616	Roo, Ana B y Cabezas				Justo P 'y G. Lynch	1786	3	1
2619	Rooney, James				Jane Lynch			1
2631	Rorke, Andrew						1	1
2630	Rorke, Mary			2631	Patrick Lynch	1844		1
1937	Royse, Abraham F			1938	Janet Jeanette Lynch	c.1830		1
2303	Royse, Mary	10 Sep 1738	1 Oct 1826	2304	John O'Flaherty	18 Jul 1764	1	1
1938	Royse, Thomas						1	1
2304	Royse, Thomas (Rev)						1	1
1247	Rushe, ???				??? Fallon		1	1
1248	Rushe?, James P? (Rev)			1247				
1980	Rushworth, Charles P.						1	1
1979	Rushworth, Horatia A.		1859	1980	M. Lynch-Staunton	1851	2	1
260	Ryan, Anne 'Annie' T	c 1899		254				
1147	Ryan, Bridget		8 May 1908		Patrick Kearney		1	
258	Ryan, Bridget	c 1889		254				
1156	Ryan, Catherine		12 May 1925		Richard Kearney		1	1
3030	Ryan, Clement Ignatius				Marie B. Maguire			1
642	Ryan, George						1	1
278	Ryan, John	c.1810	c.1870/c.60y	349	Winifred? ZZ?	c.1839	1	1
220	Ryan, Margaret	c 1882	11 Dec 1933	254	John 'Jack' Farrell	21 Feb 1906	4	1
641	Ryan, Margaret			642	Stephen Grehan		1	1
254	Ryan, Martin	c.1841	c.1908/c.67y	278	Catherine ZZ?	c.1880	4	1
2670	Ryan, Mary				Bartholomew Cooke		1	1

Num	Name	Birth date	Died	Father	Spouse	Married	Ch	M
259	Ryan, Mary Anne	c 1894		254				
349	Ryan, Mathias	c 1780					1	1
168	Ryder, Glen		c 1985		A. O'Flaherty	c 1982		1
1794	Salisbury, Sibyl of				John the Marshal		2	1
2116	Sarsfield, Catherine			2118	William McNamara		1	1
2118	Sarsfield, Francis						1	1
2144	Sarsfield, James 'Earl		1718	2137				
2137	Sarsfield, Patrick E.		bef 1695	2138	Honora '. Burke	c.1691	1	1
2138	Sarsfield, William				Anne O'Moore		1	1
1889	Scott, Thomas Augustus	1839			Sarah Jane Lynch			1
3149	Scrope, Mary	1585	1610		Thomas 'More' Moore		1	1
630	Seagrave, Clarinda			631	Marcus Blake Lynch	1796	6	1
631	Seagrave, John						1	1
1624	Serna, Celia y de la L		1965		Ernesto '. Guevara	1927	1	1
468	Shanahan, Madeleine				Charles Fallon			1
2130	Shirley, Lettice				William (7th Burke		1	1
169	Simpson, David				A. O'Flaherty	29 May 2004		1
2026	Skerrett, ???			2027	Oliver Athy			1
2290	Skerrett, ???			2291	William Lynch			1
1665	Skerrett, Anna			1664	Nicholas Tuite	1730		1
2882	Skerrett, Catherine				Patrick French		1	1
2932	Skerrett, Dominick		bef 1803		Mary Deane		3	1
1732	Skerrett, Dominick f.							
2936	Skerrett, Eleanor			2932	Thomas Lynch		1	1
2027	Skerrett, John						1	1
2234	Skerrett, John				Jane Martin			1
1713	Skerrett, John fitz							
2931	Skerrett, Magdalen			2932	George Taaffe		1	1
2291	Skerrett, Marcus ?						1	1
1640	Skerrett, Mary			1641	Peter Lynch		2	1
2451	Skerrett, Mary				John Bodkin		2	1
2934	Skerrett, Peter			2932	Mary Browne or Lynch			1
1664	Skerrett, Robert				Catherine Lynch	1 Jun 1712	1	1
1641	Skerrett, Thomas				Mary Lynch		1	1
2126	Smith, Anne				Michael (10th Burke	19 Sep 1714	1	1
833	Smith, Hatton			834	Francis Lynch-Blosse		2	1
834	Smith, John						1	1
227	Smyth, Catherine '.	c.1857	c.1928/c.71y	261	John Leahy	20 Feb 1882	5	1
297	Smyth, James	c 1894		277				
2062	Smyth, James John		13 Jan 1943	3013	Maureen Wilson Lynch	8 Jun 1935		1
1194	Smyth, John							
295	Smyth, John	c 1891		277				
276	Smyth, John 'Jack'	c 1855		261				
3013	Smyth, John Joseph						1	1
1162	Smyth, Martin Joseph			1146				
261	Smyth, Michael	c.1817	c.1901-1911	313	??? Hawkins	c.1840	3	1
294	Smyth, Michael	c 1888		277				
1146	Smyth, Patrick				Bridget '. Kearney	c.1875	1	1
299	Smyth, Patrick	c 1902		277				
298	Smyth, Thomas	c 1898		277				
296	Smyth, William	c 1893		277				
277	Smyth, William 'Bill'	c 1843		261	Mary ZZ?	c 1887	6	1
313	Smyth, William ?	c 1785			??? Walsh	c 1815	1	1
1896	Soote, George G				Alice Victoria Lynch			1
1380	St George, Miss				Martin Lynch			1
2243	St Martin, George A.	2 Mar 1831	20 Jan 1835	2190				
2694	Stanley, James				Mary Lynch			1
1910	Stapleton, Edward T.				Ellen Lynch	1855		1
1693	Staunton, George		1733	1697	Anne Lynch	1701	1	1
1697	Staunton, George			1709	Elizabeth '. Martin		1	1
1709	Staunton, George		c.1670		Eleanor Lynch		1	1
1691	Staunton, George (Col)	c 1701	3 May 1781/80y	1693	Margaret Leonard		2	1
1914	Staunton, George L	1737	14 Jan 1801	1691	Jane Collins		1	1

Num	Name	Birth date	Died	Father	Spouse	Married	Ch	M
1987	Staunton, George T	26 May 1781	Aug 1859	1914				
1690	Staunton, Lucy Barbara		1791	1691	Richard W. Cormick		1	1
430	Staunton, Mary	1848		434	James Walsh	11 Feb 1878	2	1
434	Staunton, Patrick	1804	13 Apr 1874/70		Anne ZZ?		1	1
353	Sterling, Michael							
2242	Stimpson, Sophia	abt 1835			John Robert Martin	27 Sep 1855		1
3014	Stirton, Andrew (Capt)						1	1
1886	Stirton, Emily E.	c.1824	1 May 1902/78y	3014	Edward Patk Lynch		6	1
2426	Stoker, Abraham	1799	10 Oct 1876		Charlotte M Thornley	1844	1	1
2428	Stoker, Abraham 'Bram'	8 Nov 1847	20 Apr 1912	2426	Florence Balcombe	1878		1
897	Stokes, Annie		Oct 1925		Henry Lynch-Blosse	Apr 1881		1
2139	Stuart, James (1st D.	21 Aug 1670	12 Jun 1734	2140	Honora '. Burke	26 Mar 1695		1
2140	Stuart, James II	14 Oct 1633	16 Sep 1701		Arabella Churchill	1665	1	1
1130	Sullivan, Barbara			1127	Peter Long	c 2003		1
1128	Sullivan, Colm			1127	Cecilia Broome	10 Nov 2007		1
1132	Sullivan, Michael			1127	Mairin Conneely	c 1998		1
1127	Sullivan, Thomas				Bridget '. Conneely		3	1
991	Sutherland, Cara Lynne			992	Richard Lynch-Blosse	18 Sep 1976	2	1
992	Sutherland, George L						1	1
2042	Taaffe, E				Eleanor Athy			1
2930	Taaffe, George				Magdalen Skerrett		1	1
2708	Taaffe, Julia		c.1875	2930	Peter Lynch	1832	6	1
1677	Talbot, Anna Eliza M.			1678	Thomas N Redington	1842	1	1
2312	Talbot, Elinor ? E.	1613	abt 1650		Theobold (3rd Burke	aft Sep 163	4	1
1678	Talbot, John Hyacinth						1	1
2128	Talbot, Mary				John (9th E. Burke	Oct 1684	1	1
1879	Taylor, Caroline			1880	Henry (Capt) Lynch	Aug 1838	4	1
1880	Taylor, Robert (Col)						1	1
327	Taylores, Bella ?							
2427	Thornley, Charlotte M	28 Jun 1818	1901	2432	Abraham Stoker	1844	1	1
2432	Thornley, Thomas				Matilda Blake	3 Oct 1817	2	1
2431	Thornley, Thomas Blake	1822	1850	2432				
1393	Tighe, Rosina		1873	1374	Thomas Lynch	14 Jul 1828	5	1
1374	Tighe, Thomas						1	2
69	Toole, Anne 'Nan T.	c 1881	1 Dec 1951	70	James 'Rua' McDonagh	c.1902	2	1
537	Toole, Martin	c 1805					1	1
70	Toole, Michael	c.1839		537	Mary 'Adley' Audley	24 Feb 1867	1	1
1427	Trant, Alice			1428	Stephen Lynch		2	1
1428	Trant, Edward						1	1
3096	Treacy, ?				? Burke		1	1
3097	Treacy, Noel 'TD'			3096				
1551	Trench, Thomas				??? Lynch			1
1666	Tuite, Nicholas				Anna Skerrett	1730		1
3103	Tyrell, Cecilia				Thomas Blosse		2	1
2389	Tyrell, Edward		May 1713		??? O'Flaherty			1
2961	Usher, Catherine				Francis Darcy		1	1
1783	Vale, Agnes 'de'				John M. Lynch			1
1929	Varenne, G (Rev Dr)						1	1
1928	Varenne, Georgina			1929	Richard Marcus Lynch		1	1
382	Varley, Margaret				Thomas Lyons		1	1
2660	Vaughan, Alice				Henry Charles Lynch		8	1
2481	Vesey, ???			2482			2	1
2186	Vesey, Elizabeth	c.1758	bef 1796	2187	Richard '. Martin	Feb 1777	3	1
2187	Vesey, George	c 1732		2481			1	1
2482	Vesey, John	1638	28 Mar 1716				1	1
2480	Vesey, John (Rev)			2481	Elizabeth Lynch			1
1645	Vigo, ? 'of Leinster'						1	1
1644	Vigo, Margaret			1645	Peter 'Pierce' Lynch		1	1
2124	Vincent, Hester Amelia				John Smith Burke	1 Jul 1740	1	1
981	Walker, Edith Caroline		20 Jan 1953	965	Edward Lynch-Blosse	11 Dec 1883	5	1
965	Walker, George Alfred						2	1
964	Walker, Mary C.		10 Sep 1936	965	Robert Lynch-Blosse	6 Dec 1881	1	1
1972	Wallscourt, Johanna				Richard Burke		1	1

An extract from the database of 2843 individuals (1 October 2013) including the Anglo-Norman Lynches who settled in Galway and members of my extended family (PaulBMcNulty.com on http://www.myfamily) (Ch = number of children; M = number of marriages).

Num	Name	Birth date	Died	Father	Spouse	Married	Ch	M
314	Walsh, ???				William ? Smyth	c 1815	1	1
3112	Walsh, Colman	c.1860	Apr-Jun 1930		Bridget Connolly	c.1890	1	1
429	Walsh, James	c 1840		436	Mary Staunton	11 Feb 1878	2	1
3110	Walsh, John	21? May 189	18? Aug 1962	3112	Nora McDonagh	9 Apr 1939	1	1
3111	Walsh, Kathleen	18 Feb 1941		3110				
431	Walsh, Martin		21 Apr 1983	429				
106	Walsh, Mary	2 Oct 1938		422	Thomas Fallon	1972	7	1
433	Walsh, Mary							
422	Walsh, Michael		2 Dec 1963	429	Honoria Greavey	8 Apr 1916	1	2
1237	Walsh, Mrs							
419	Walsh, Nuala				??? Connolly		1	1
436	Walsh, Patrick		bef 1878/32y		Margaret? ZZ?		1	1
2559	Walsh, Timothy 'Tim'				Catherine '. Lynch			1
600	Warren, Garrett				Anne Lynch			1
1144	Whelan, Patrick				Mary Teresa Kearney			1
1926	Williams, George A				Helen Grace			1
2060	Wilson, David John		18 Apr 1864	1686	Mary Kirwan			1
1685	Wilson, Ellen	1794	1878	1686	Patrick Marcus Lynch	1820	8	1
1686	Wilson, John						2	1
3027	Wilson-Wright, John			3028	Sheila G. Lynch	30 Jun 1953		1
3028	Wilson-Wright, Leonard						1	1
1917	Wood, Charlotte Brock			1918	Henry Lynch-Staunton	1838	1	1
1918	Wood, John Brock						1	1
3019	Yate, Charles Edwd						1	1
3018	Yate, Lois Burnley			3019	Henry Pk (Col) Lynch	11 Apr 1931	2	1
1633	Zaldivar, Carmen de y				Estanislao 'y Lynch		1	1
1618	Zavaleta, Maria y R.				Patrick 'P J y Lynch	1813	2	1
2954	ZZ?, ?				John Lynch		1	1
3136	ZZ?, ?				James '. McDonough		1	1
3154	ZZ?, ?				John Bodkin		1	1
2512	ZZ?, Anastacia '.						1	1
435	ZZ?, Anne				Patrick Staunton		1	1
59	ZZ?, Anne 'Annie'				Owen McCauley		1	1
148	ZZ?, Barbara R				Timothy J. McHugh		2	1
1426	ZZ?, Bridget				Stephen Lynch		2	1
510	ZZ?, Bridget	c 1855			Thomas Greaney	c 1888	1	1
255	ZZ?, Catherine	c 1850			Martin Ryan	c.1880	4	1
2875	ZZ?, Christina '.				Robert '. French		2	1
2923	ZZ?, Deborah		bef Mar 1766		Martin Lynch			1
1024	ZZ?, Dorothy?				Michael F (Dr) Cox		1	1
1734	ZZ?, Gyles or Julia				Viscount David Barry		1	2
195	ZZ?, Hannah	c 1805	4 Jul 1873/68y		John McColgan	c.1830	2	1
1821	ZZ?, Hawise				Robert 'de' Quenci		1	1
1008	ZZ?, Helena				Michael (1st Bellew		2	1
2963	ZZ?, Honoria		bef 1795		Neptune Lynch		6	1
2928	ZZ?, James 'Jacobo'							
2748	ZZ?, Jane				Joseph Lynch			1
673	ZZ?, Janetta				Arthur Lynch		1	1
1135	ZZ?, Joan				John Fallon	1948	3	1
1774	ZZ?, Juliane				Dominick '. Lynch			1
145	ZZ?, Leilani				Timothy McHugh	c 1984	1	1
3091	ZZ?, Lucy				Lenny Connaughton			1
1016	ZZ?, Margaret				Francis ? Norman		1	1
2554	ZZ?, Margaret				Joseph Cooke			1
2956	ZZ?, Margaret				George Browne		1	1
31	ZZ?, Margaret				James? Boylan		1	1
34	ZZ?, Margaret				James Kavanagh		1	1
437	ZZ?, Margaret?				Patrick Walsh		1	1
188	ZZ?, Mary				Colman '. McDonagh		1	1
245	ZZ?, Mary	c 1751			??? Farrell	c 1785	1	1
2548	ZZ?, Mary	c.1838			Michael Lynch	c.1870/73	3	1
293	ZZ?, Mary	c 1864			William 'Bill' Smyth	c 1887	6	1
3132	ZZ?, Mary				James Jos McDonough		2	1

An extract from the database of 2843 individuals (1 October 2013) including the Anglo-Norman Lynches who settled in Galway and members of my extended family (PaulBMcNulty.com on http://www.myfamily) (Ch = number of children; M = number of marriages).

Num	Name	Birth date	Died	Father	Spouse	Married	Ch	M
414	ZZ?, Mary			139	??? 'Bourke' Burke			1
891	ZZ?, Mary				Edmund 'en T. Lynch		1	1
3108	ZZ?, Mary?				Patrick Farrell			1
33	ZZ?, Nora	c.1819	c.1899		Thaddeus McHugh		4	1
1004	ZZ?, Olivia				Christopher Bellew		1	1
191	ZZ?, Patrick	c.1887	30 Dec 1893					
1043	ZZ?, Sebina		1832		Thomas Morris		1	1
279	ZZ?, Winifred?	c.1803	13 Jul 1868/65		John Ryan	c.1839	1	1

ABOUT THE AUTHOR

PAUL B MCNULTY

I write historical novels based on real events in 18th century Ireland. My apprenticeship in writing commenced at University College Dublin where I edited an engineering magazine, *The Anvil*. Afflicted with wanderlust, I travelled west to Ohio State and MIT to continue my studies to master's and doctoral level. While in Boston, my interest in history unfolded through participation in the Committee for Justice in Northern Ireland and in the anti-Vietnam war movement. On return to Ireland, I honed my writing skills, publishing scientific papers as well as writing on food-related issues in the popular media.

Following a career in Biosystems Engineering at UCD, I revisited my historical interest by studying 'The genealogy of the Anglo-Norman Lynches who settled in Galway.' The consequent discovery of a treasure-trove of forgotten Irish stories inspired me to write *Spellbound by Sibella*, a finalist in the 2012 William Faulkner Novel Competition. My debut novel deals with the turbulent romance between Irish beauty, Sibella Cottle and the rakish Sir Harry Lynch-Blosse of Mayo. Critiques from a writer's group, The Corner Table, of which I am a founding member, guide my writing.

I am at an advanced stage in my second novel, *The Abduction of Anne O'Donel*, a finalist in the 2013 William Faulkner Novel Competition. My third novel, *The Bloody Bodkins,* is at an earlier stage of development. It explores the possibility that a man may have been hanged for a crime he did not commit.

I live in Dublin with my wife, Treasa Ní Chonaola. We have three children, Dara, Nora and Meabh, and a grandchild, Lily Marie. I derive inspiration from the wild splendour of Mayo and Connemara. My website address is http://paul-mcnulty.com.